"Both scholarly and deeply personal, this is essential reading for anyone ready to confront the silences around gender, power and the Black woman's identity in the Caribbean – 'Butch Heterosexuality' redefines black femininity through the lens of resistance, survival and historical truth".

Anya A. A. Lorde, *Attorney-at-Law (Family Law), Barbados Bar*

"*Butch Heterosexuality* is an important contribution to scholarship in several areas – gender studies, post-colonial studies, Caribbean history. Marsha Myrie Obi has written a beautiful book that weaves together personal narrative and Caribbean social and political thought to present the case for a unique kind of women's resistance to gendered and colonial oppression. Myrie Obi offers 'butch heterosexuality' as a term for a certain kind of refusal enacted by women in plantation societies. By rejecting what is a compulsory femininity for heterosexuality, women have reclaimed some of the freedom over their bodies. On the plantations, masculinity was practised by slave women as a matter of survival, as a way of demonstrating strength and utility and also in effort to avoid unwanted sexual attention. Myrie Obi explains 'butch heterosexuality as a legitimate way that Caribbean women refused the boundaries of creole society… [it can] now be harnessed by those of us women who enjoy sex with men but who refuse to live in relationships of subordination where our mental health, financial well-being and sexual and physical safety are not guaranteed'. She argues, with compelling evidence and conviction, that the survival strategies of black women during slavery 'ratooned' their way into the modern era and manifest today as socio-political, gendered refusals. Ultimately, understanding performances of masculinity and femininity in colonial context is important for interrogating transnational and interpersonal power relations and moving towards equality and peace, and away from subordination. This is a brilliant book that should be read by anyone interested in the politics of gender and race".

Candace Johnson, *professor, Department of Political Science, University of Guelph, Ontario*

"Marsha Myrie Obi's debut book moves us through historical gender readings of the Commonwealth Caribbean; offers theoretical analysis; and provides moving, though melancholy personal stories, that colour this assessment of expectations, performances and rebellious being that characterize Black womanhood/the feminine in the region. Myrie Obi's evaluation of colonial, raced and trauma informed patriarchy; compliance with it; and resistance against shakes the reader asking them to pause and reflect. A brave, thought provoking, moving and likely contentious take on gender in the Commonwealth Caribbean that is well worth reading!"

Kristina Hinds, *PhD, senior lecturer in political science, The University of the West Indies, Cave Hill, social commentator, author, and firebrand*

"Dr. Myrie Obi's analysis is sharp and deeply historically – and personally – contextualized. Illuminating how some Black Caribbean women's performances of gender enable resistance to individualized and systemic patriarchal oppressions, *Butch Heterosexuality* also provides a critical conceptualization of gender – as system, as strategy, as identity-in-practice – that will be valuable to readers in many parts of the world".

Elizabeth Jackson, *PhD, Director, Community Engaged Scholarship Institute, University of Guelph, Ontario*

Butch Heterosexuality in Black Caribbean Womanhood

This critical text proposes new ways of conceptualizing Black womanhood by challenging plantation patriarchal culture and its binary constructions, and methods of Black heterosexual coupling. Black Women's performances of womanhood are understood from juxtapositions with white idealism, resulting in Black womanhood explained negatively or for what it is not, rather than positively and expansively for what it is and could be.

This book contextualizes Black womanhood as it was shaped by historical experiences of plantation, trauma, survival and most importantly, triumph. Myrie Obi expands upon her theory of butch heterosexuality, which identifies elements of gender presentation commonly marked as masculine. Using Jack Halberstam's essential work of queer theory, "Female Masculinity" as a jumping off point, Myrie Obi uses the Commonwealth Caribbean as a site of new inquiry. Butch heterosexuality challenges the patriarchal gender binary and encourages an understanding of sexuality and gender performance as distinct, arguing against a conflation of female masculinity and lesbianism. The result is an alternative way to start conversations about decolonial approaches to understanding (Caribbean) Black women, Black sexuality and Black gender performances.

This book is critical reading for scholar activists and students in the areas of Black or Caribbean studies, Black sexualities and Gender studies, sociology, social work, politics, gender justice and social justice courses.

Marsha Myrie Obi, PhD, is a Caribbean researcher, whose research explores the intersections of womanism, Black studies, philosophy as praxis and intellectual history. She works with embedding anti-oppressive and inclusive pedagogies in predominantly White institutions and is an adjunct professor in Political Science at the University of Guelph, Ontario, Canada. She is the master advocate in the survivor-led group Operation Safe Space in Barbados.

Leading Conversations on Black Sexualities and Identities

Series editors: James C. Wadley

Leading Conversations on Black Sexualities and Identities aims to stimulate sensitive conversations and teachings surrounding Black sexuality. Written by academics and practitioners who have dedicated their work to the distinctive sexual and relational experiences of persons of African descent, the series aims to provoke an enhanced understanding throughout the field of sexology and identify educational and clinical strategies for change. Amplifying issues and voices often minimalized and marginalized, this series is a continuation and expansion of inquiry and advocacy upon the complexities and nuances of relational negotiation, identity affirmation, critical discourse, and liberated sexual expression.

Titles in the series:

Sex Positivity and White-Sex Supremacy: Ending Complicity in Black Body Erasure
Carole Clements

Black Women, Intersectionality, and Workplace Bullying: Intersecting Distress
Leah P. Hollis

The Colonization of Black Sexualities: A Clinical Guide to Relearning and Healing
Anne Mauro

Black Women's Bodily Autonomy, Sexual Freedom, and Pleasure: Explorations of the Hot Girl Movement
Clarissa E. Francis

Butch Heterosexuality in Black Caribbean Womanhood: Exploring Gender Performance and Sexuality
Marsha Myrie Obi

Butch Heterosexuality in Black Caribbean Womanhood

Exploring Gender Performance and Sexuality

Marsha Myrie Obi

Routledge
Taylor & Francis Group
NEW YORK AND LONDON

First published 2026
by Routledge
605 Third Avenue, New York, NY 10158

and by Routledge
4 Park Square, Milton Park, Abingdon, Oxon, OX14 4RN

Routledge is an imprint of the Taylor & Francis Group, an informa business

ISBN: 9781032855691 (hbk)
ISBN: 9781032844411 (pbk)
ISBN: 9781003518709 (ebk)

DOI: 10.4324/9781003518709

Typeset in Times New Roman
by codeMantra

To Ochi Layne

I hope you are the kind of man who embraces strength in your woman and finds the strength to reject patriarchy to keep her safe.

I say a huge thank you to Prof. James Wadley for recognizing that this work was a book and for making that possible, and to Julia Giordano who is, hands down the best editor in the world.

Too often we forget the waiters and the care workers who make things as time-consuming as writing a book possible. Romaine Heldt, thank you...to you and the faceless crew for fixing my crown and my grammar, and carrying me into the final stages of this work.

Contents

Foreword xi
Preface xiii

Introduction 1
What Womanhood and Which Caribbean? 2
Methodological Approaches 4
Barbados and the CC: Ratoons of Gender 9
1600 – Legal Emancipation first Ratooning 10
Legal Emancipation to 1930s Uprisings second Ratooning 12
1930s Uprisings to Independence third Ratooning 14
The Chapters 15

1 **The Creation of Plantation** 18
White Men and Plantation 20
Plantocratic Patriarchal Culture 20
Effect of PPC on Marriage 22
Black Men and Plantation 24
Black Men and Individualistic Patriarchy 25
Black Men and Labour 27
Polygamy or Dysfunction? 28
White Women and Plantation 30
Black Women and Plantation 32
Phibbah the Businesswoman 33
Conclusion 38

2 Breaking Silence: State/Family Dysfunction and Plantation 42
Individualistic Patriarchy and State Formation 43
Individualistic Patriarchy and Caribbean Nationalism 47
Strong Women and Caribbean Society 48
State Mechanics, Women and Men 54
A Case Study 56
Conclusion 61

3 Butch Heterosexuality: Black Women Are (Gender) Innovators 64
Reconciling Race 65
Black, Trauma-Informed Partnership 70
Rethinking Gender Justice and Theory 73
Rethinking the State – Nationalism Reclaimed 75
Conclusion 81

4 Redefining Heterosexual Partnership: Building Anti-Patriarchal Relationships by Prioritizing Healing 84

Works Cited *105*
Index *111*

Foreword

James C. Wadley, PhD July 2025

Dr. Marsha Hinds Myrie and I began correspondence approximately 18 months ago when she asked me to consider her manuscript to be published in the *Journal of Black Sexuality and Relationships (JBSR)* (University of Nebraska Press). At the time, there were a few double issues of the JBSR that were to be published over the next year or so I asked Marsha if she might be interested in taking a different path towards publication. I shared with her that Routledge (Taylor &Francis) offered and created space for authors to submit manuscripts to the Leading Conversations about Black Sexualities and Identities series where they could extend the work that they've already done into a "mini-book". Marsha took some time to think through the offer, and she agreed to share her work with our community with this book.

I am honoured and happy to work with this talented professional who provides language and voice to the gender and sexual identities of Caribbean Black women who seek individual and relational empowerment. Butch heterosexuality subverts the dominant gender expression paradigm that suggests that women should present in a particular manner. Marsha offers light upon continuum of sexual expression and provides us with historic, cultural, relational and gendered examples of how some Black women negotiate roles and expectations across various communities. Her scholarly narrative feels personable and rich as it connects the past and present understandings about race and gender constructions. Dr. Myrie then uses these analyses to shed light upon and sculpts future discourse about Caribbean women's relationships with themselves and their partners. This book embraces and expounds upon the work of Black womanist theorists, and Marsha helps us to think critically about how we conceptualize and talk about gender in formal and informal spaces.

I am positive that you will enjoy reading this book and using it as a tool for discussion with your students, peers and colleagues.

Preface

Author's Note: I start this work with an offering of some of the most important bit of who I am. This is the way that all academic or academic adjacent work should start because there is no knowledge without value judgement, there is no knowing without bias and there is no analysis without being positioned. So that you can care yourself while reading this work, let me declare early that it includes tough conversations about tough topics. There are descriptions of sexual abuse and the struggle of abuse that affect the lives of women and girls. One characteristic of the way that I always do my work is to be accessible and available. My email is mhmhindsmy@uoguelph.ca and I am happy if you reach out as a part of caring yourself. I hope that in your circle of support there is an office mate or a friend who can support you as you read. I hope you can discuss with your parent/safe adult/guardian. I especially hope that if you are partnered this book features in a date night. Finally, if you are working with a therapist or other care worker, this reading becomes a session or two or whatever.

COVID-19 is beginning to feel like a distant memory. Other events leading to loss of life and despair – man made and natural – have moved our attention beyond COVID. There is a lot to keep the minds and emotions of Caribbean people engaged: Super hurricanes like Beryl (the earliest category five hurricane to form on record thus far), Debby, Helene and Milton (which challenged the First World resolve of Florida); genocide in Palestine; continued foreign interference in Ayiti and the perrenial destabilization and pilferage in Africa. COVID-19, and perhaps the sustained grief that our modern world causes, is largely responsible for this book. Before COVID-19, I was busy mothering and building my career. Then during the pandemic I existed on pure adrenaline. I was the president of the National Organization of Women in Barbados and I went right into leveraging contacts to prepare and deliver food stock for mainly single mothers, who due to their loss of employment found themselves struggling to feed their children. I was also making sure that police and other stakeholders in Barbados understood that they had to take gender-based violence broadly and intimate partner violence specifically, seriously during the lockdowns.

For the first part of movement restrictions in Barbados I flatly broke the law to work with women and girls in delivering hampers, mediating challenges and providing support with filing protection orders. The Government of Barbados created a panel of stakeholders to discuss their pandemic response strategy which excluded civil society. Of course, supermarkets and the business sector were represented at the table, the church, police and health sectors but the sector with day-to-day responsibility for the response to gender-based violence – civil society – was absent from the conversation. Why would women's groups be invited to a serious national table of decision making? The general sentiment about women's organizations in Barbados is that advocates are, after all, a few troublemaking 'feminists' who created gender wars and keep unnecessary noise in public media. To my recollection, the official government passes were never granted to facilitate the work throughout communities in Barbados, but I was also never stopped or confronted for flouting the stay-in-place laws. This kind of existence beyond the law and beyond legitimation is a feature of plantation society which Commonwealth Caribbean (CC) women know well.

I dealt with the fear and grief of the COVID-19 pandemic after the lockdowns were lifted. I became intensely lonely, and I kept feeling as though if I had died in the pandemic I would have been a huge burden to my biological children. I thought of my still relatively young children at that time having to identify and manage my mortal remains. I also thought about potentially being at home and ill for days without anyone recognizing. I had a sudden urge for love and true to the observation of bell hooks in *All About Love* the only kind of love I could conjure was romantic love (3). The prevalence of plantocratic patriarchal culture (PPC) in Barbados I fell out of the dating pool. I was clear that I was not going to find a Barbadian man whose thinking had evolved beyond the PPC ethos. I had had enough brushes with men, not just in romantic ways but in my work with women and girls to understand that there was a systemic hatred and disdain for women and girls. Barbadian men love sex, but they despise women. Black male hatred is a colonial mechanism used to weaken and dehumanize Africans kidnapped and relocated to the Caribbean. Thus, when I returned to Canada in 2021, the unprocessed emotional turmoil of COVID-19 and the desire to prove that Barbadian men were a lost, old fashioned kind of man in a modern world where men had moved on, I spent the better part of the end of 2021 actively dating.

The first semblance of a strong connection I felt with another Caribbean Diaspora soul resulted in marriage. Many people got a COVID cat or dog – I got a COVID husband! I don't know if to say, unsurprisingly it ended in divorce but that marriage was valuable to me for two reasons. First, I realized that the day it happened was a naming ceremony for me. Shanique Myrie, a Jamaican woman who sued the Government over her treatment as a CARICOM national entitled to freedom of movement under the Revised Treaty of Chaguaramas and prevailed, became a huge influence on me. It was one of the first times in my practice as a women and girls activist that I had seen a woman operate outside of the rigid class apartheid and respectability characteristic of the feminist movement in the Caribbean. Shanique forced Barbados and the state to respect her as she was – as all humans are – an imperfect human but a whole human deserving of her rights. It so happens that my marriage came with the opportunity of having Myrie as a surname and I made it clear that I was keeping the name regardless of what happened because of its significance to me. What I thought was a wedding was actually a naming ritual.

The second experience that was important about my COVID husband was his reflections on me and what fuelled the squabbles between us. He thought I did not dress feminine enough and I did not 'behave like a woman'. There is a very public and widespread polemic between Black men and Black women about who is the more difficult and at fault party in the failure of intimate relationships in our community. In response to my COVID husband's observations it would perhaps have been easier to join the noise about the uselessness of Black men if I were not simultaneously raising three boys into Black men – the universe has something of a sense of humour! I have seen firsthand how the verbal brutality of Black mothers has incapacitated their sons (hooks 61). I was purposeful as a mother not to do the same to my sons. Instead of joining in the chorus of complaint, I was willing to think about other answers in response to my COVID husband's observations – other answers for the patterns that have challenged my ability to coexist with Black men. That reflection resulted in this book. To explain myself I began thinking about my grandmother and how I was raised. I don't know if what I have come up with would be a satisfactory answer for my COVID husband, but I will forever be grateful to him for the part he played in my naming journey – both a surname I treasure and this new identity – butch heterosexual that I have claimed for myself. As I rummaged through the laments of my COVID husband what follows in these pages is what I have learnt about myself and the legacy that created me.

I am a Black (read Diasporic African) woman whose family settled between Barbados and Canada. My great-grandmother, Beatrice Hollingsworth, was one of the first land-owning women in the parish of St. Lucy, Barbados. I grew up on her several acres of land with my grandmother and an extramarital child of my grandmother's brother. My grandfather returned home literally to be taken care of as he died, but other than that it was us three women. I ran in the fields with my cousins and I nurtured animals. I also understood very early on that hard work had the reward of being left alone. I think both organically and at the instruction of my grandmother I learnt the importance of financial independence for a woman. Beatrice's daughter, my grandmother, Eulease Hinds, raised pigs as her major source of income. In modern business one of the 'best practices' is to ensure value added so that the merchant makes the maximum amount of profit. My grandmother was the primary source of that lesson for me. She hired the butcher to 'stick' her pigs and disembowel them. He was then to cut the carcass into manageable bits for her. She took over from there and what that ensured was that she paid him for two hours as opposed to the entire day. That lesson is cemented because of the weeklong negotiation it always took to have the butcher come out for 'piece work' and not 'day's work'. Next, she sold her pigs as prime cuts of meat but she also sold the delicacy Black pudding and souse. Finally, she made lard and fats and other fringe dishes which the household used for weeks after the slaughter. Thus, the only thing discarded from the pig was teeth and skin. My granny's business was not steeped in a capitalist model. She extended credit to trusted customers and free door-to-door delivery – the footwork of my cousin and me. There were some people in the village that my granny cared – Ms. Baker – her old friend who lived alone and eventually lost her foot to the dreaded diabetes and others whose pudding and souse was free and who also received other meals during the week. My granny was a Ubuntu philosopher and an obeah woman. She knew what every bush was good for and she knew the value of living with and in community.

Eulease was a strong and undaunted woman. She had moved back to her mother's land to flee an abusive and alcoholic husband. In retrospect, our status as land-owning middle, if not upper-class entrepreneurial women allowed my grandmother to escape her husband and live a life that was not available to most working-class women in the Caribbean either at that time in what would have been the 70s and 80s or indeed in contemporary Barbados. Eulease used the business acumen passed from Beatrice to start her pig farming and to run her business successfully. She had the land resources to build her own house and sons and a brother who provided emotional support and sweat labour. The audacity and tenacity of the Hollingsworth women are as embedded in our DNA as our high cheekbones and our propensity to find ourselves in abusive relationships with men. My grandfather, from whom granny fled, sexually abused his daughter and in turn, his son, my father, sexually abused me. The licks my grandfather rained on his wife also rained on his children. I think this testimony is important to expand the spectre of family violence in the Caribbean beyond a working-class experience. My personal story is not a secret or unusual one. Available literature in all kinds of genres about family and childhood in the Caribbean (and its related Diasporas) outlines the levels and kinds of abuse (Shorter Brown 76–77, 113, 151, 199, 289; Spencer Gibbs 69, 151, 172; Vasconcellos 5–7; Lorde 18 & 65; Downing 56 & 73). Abuse in Caribbean families is not just physical – although there is enough of that. There is a significant element of psychological abuse – abandonment, secrecy, gaslighting and manipulation, sexual and financial abuse.

There are many things I later understood about my grandmother that required my tempering of the hero-tinted glasses I saw her with. She was a shrewd businesswoman. At the same time she was cooking extra and feeding indigent people in the community she was also making sure she got the most for her meat and the delicacies she made. I later learnt that those free offerings to elderly people may have had a price tag after all. The family is scrutinizing some of the deals that left my great-grandmother and grandmother as two significant landholders. I also realize the brutality in her 'discipline' that I was spared but that I saw inflicted on other family members. Audre Lorde, in *Zami: A New Spelling of My Name*, captures some of the harmful ways that Caribbean women have used physical punishment and harsh words to manage feelings of hopelessness, lack of control and an inability to be vulnerable (Lorde 12,58,63-65). Notwithstanding, I find myself constantly returning to my grandmother's approach to womanhood because I believe that this performance of womanhood is one that holds a specific historical place in the experience of displacement and survival of CC Black women. The performance of womanhood I saw in my great-grandmother and grandmother has irrevocably shaped my own performance of womanhood. Rightfully then as I reflected on my COVID husband's summation of me, my source of understanding womanhood was central to understanding myself. My grandmother took on many of the characteristics Lorde describes of her own mother and certainly, like many other Caribbean women of their time. Their attributes defied traditional views (read White Western) and expectations of womanhood (Lorde 12,58,63-65) (Lorde 15-17). This book is inspired by reflections. It is very much me trying to find language for the ways that I have recovered and reconstructed my womanhood into something that makes sense to me and which I want to live inside and navigate.

Introduction

What kind of place is the Caribbean specifically in the context of gender? The general sentiment among men in Barbados and the Commonwealth Caribbean (CC) is that gender is an import directly related to feminism and women's liberation and it is ill-suited to the Caribbean or causes 'gender wars'. The sentiment is in various ways replicated in scholarship on gender (Miller 76; Watson, "The Globalization of the Discourse on Gender and Its Impacts on the Caribbean" 55(a)). Many women are unwilling to discuss the matters for fear of being labelled feminist or troublemaking. However, the truth is, gender is as old as plantation and the wider colonial enterprise itself and was a significant part of structuring the uneven power relations undergirding the proto-capitalist/plantation society. Hilary Beckles writes, "the linking of white womanhood and Black womanhood to freedom and slavery respectively meant that the entire ideological fabric of the slave system was conceived in terms of race, sex **and gender**" (Beckles, "Sex and Gender in the Historiography of Caribbean Slavery" 131). I agree with Beckles that gender is not a synonym for sex or biological difference nor I would add women's liberation in the contemporary moment ("Sex and Gender in the Historiography of Caribbean Slavery" 127). Gender is a tool of colonial domination that was critical to preserving hierarchical stratification that is the fulcrum of Caribbean plantation society. It was gender and not sex that differentiated white and Black women. The continued embrace of traditional, rigid gender norms in the CC held and continue to hold women outside freedom.

Black motherhood is both a historical and contemporary example of unfreedom. The Black womb was critical in reproducing unfree labour (134–5). To guard their wombs, their peace of mind and their souls, Black women honed characteristics that marked Black womanhood including independence and strength. For instance, while there is the general view that women's movements were restricted on plantations, white society viewed Black women as property and restrictions on their movement had more to do with ensuring they were not lost to production and less to do with Black women being conceptualized as needing protection. Thus Black women used their freedom of movement in strategic and defiant ways. In fact, autonomy and freedom of

DOI: 10.4324/9781003518709-1

movement became the bedrocks of a type of femininity that I argue emerges out of Black women's experience of slavery in the CC. Female masculinity help us to rethink and understand Caribbean women's approaches to performances of womanhood. It has been and continues to offer useful gender performances for CC women. There are large gaps in material available about the lives of women in the CC, but there are some substantial contributions in the work of Lucille Mair (1987), Hilary Beckles (1989) and others. I hope that this contribution can encourage more research and writing on Caribbean women as whole beings, the society in which they live/d understood and negotiate/d gender and not just in relation to their children or relationships. Two other observations of Trouilot are important both to defining the region 'geographically' and Black performances of womanhood in it. He explains that not much in the Caribbean can be understood without consideration of its historical origins (21) and the fact that the Caribbean is unique because it is perhaps one of the oldest spaces shaped by colonialism and its logics (Trouillot 22). Hold all this in mind moving through this book. I deal with implications for understanding the Caribbean itself before returning to gender considerations.

What Womanhood and Which Caribbean?

Michel-Rolph Trouillot contends that "pronouncements of Caribbean people of various origins have long made their way into anthropological accounts with unequal value added" (25). That state of affairs obtains in most academic discipline and this book hopes to add to the literature with respect to CC women's lives. I don't just mean how women have served their communities or how they have mothered children. It is important to think about how CC women perform/ed and refuse/d to perform womanhood especially in the context of Transatlantic slave trade/plantation society brutality. Where did Caribbean women get their approaches to womanhood? Did Caribbean women seamlessly embrace Victorian values of womanhood? How much of the Caribbean approach to womanhood are African retentions? This book came about to work through one way that Black women in the region of the Caribbean – perhaps better delineated as the CC – have navigated and approached womanhood. *Butch heterosexuality*, refers to my engagement with the invitation of Jack Halberstam to write more of the history of female masculinities as well as to determine the uses of female masculinity for heterosexual women (Halberstam 268–9). It delves deeper into Audre Lorde's assertion that to understand Black (Caribbean) women requires grappling with the fact that "there have always been Black dykes around – in a sense of powerful and women-oriented women – who would rather have died than use that name for themselves" (15).

I hope butch heterosexuality conceptually (further) interrupts the sex and gender binary. It debunks the notion that women who enjoy sex with men cannot possess their own masculinity. It also refutes the conflation that once a woman is not trans or queer, the only type of womanhood she can perform is one that is "bad for your health" (Halberstam 268). Butch heterosexuality eschews a 'normal' gender performance of womanhood as one that is passive and supplementary to masculine manhood. Butch heterosexuality is a practice that truly separates gender and sex and underlines the social construction of gender. Women who enjoy sleeping with men can operate in and experience human sexuality with men and also refuse to perform womanhood within the confines of established gender roles. In fact, I contend that the Caribbean is a space replete with examples of women who did exactly this. Simplifying or overlooking this history inadvertently created confusion for both Caribbean women and men, giving rise to a gender war in the region and resulting in unhealthy heterosexual partnerships. By highlighting the intricate relationship between social experience and gender I hope to elucidate Caribbean heterosexual orientation to resistance and revolution – as strength in a way that heterosexuality is generally not imagined. This project, I hope is a manifestation of Deborah Thomas' call of the use of the historical as "both analytic category and method, a way to parse the place of the past in the present" (*Exceptional Violence* 11). I am not purporting that all Caribbean women navigate womanhood in this way or to replace scholarship that takes Caribbean womanhood in other directions. I am expanding the possible repertoires of understanding how Black women in the Caribbean seek/sought to hold onto and fight for the ultimate freedom of all – the freedom over one's own body (Sheller 54–9). Naming is important to understanding the CC as a region and the culture of its people.

The Caribbean is not homogenous and defining it improves accuracy. This book contemplates the CC – a term that it is fraught but may be the best of other problematic choices such as British Caribbean, Anglophone Caribbean or the West Indies. The Caribbean in this book is the archipelago spread between Guyana on the South American continent and Jamaica. This region is bound together by its shared history of British colonial rule, common patterns of colonial society and language and approaches to gender performance. Research in disciplines including cultural studies, linguistics and history uses Jamaica as a general metaphor for the CC. This book uses Barbados in the same way. CC legitimates comparison and analysis in this subregion but also resists conflation of the broader region that is also connected but more diverse (Ayiti, Cuba, Aruba, Bonaire, and Curacao all belong to the Caribbean differently defined). To understand the Caribbean is to simultaneously understand heterogeneity and homogeneity. I agree with historian Franklin Knight that in some cases "common experiences and understandings…outweigh the territorial differences or peculiarities" (*The Caribbean* xvi).

Concomitantly, the Caribbean is also a region constantly in flux. The changes between, for example, emancipation and nationalism and nationalism and contemporary experiences, especially in the context of gender performances should not be overlooked. Knight's assertion that "political boundaries do not necessarily make, or conform to, cultural boundaries" (*The Caribbean* xvi) is another important insight in conceptualizing the CC. Constant simultaneous shifts are necessary to accurately reflect and understand the Caribbean experience. It calls for, in my view, a unique approach to reading and knowledge making (I offer one in the methodological section below). Finally, the Caribbean has grown significant Diaspora communities in Canada, the United States and Britain, and these should not be overlooked when defining the region. Although the Diasporas exist in different political and geographical regions, the shared Caribbean culture and approaches to life remain notably congruent with the home territories. Caribbean ways of being remain puissant in the Diaspora but the Diaspora is also an area of possibility for rethinking and reshaping gender norms. Caribbean queer theory finds safer space to manifest itself in the Diaspora than home and it is through the queer critique of the gender binary and relations between and among people that heterosexual women themselves can find better possibilities for liberation and healthier relationships with men.

Methodological Approaches

Caribbean gender study is plagued with ahistoricity. Although women across the Caribbean at all levels of the society have fought for their freedom and better ways of living that are not hindered by gender boundaries, they have not had equal access to literate culture. Put another way, although CC women have lived out performances of gender that allowed them to avoid abuse and plunder, care and support their children and thrive in harsh plantation societies, other people have written their stories because they themselves could not or did not have the avenues to write. Where writing has been done it has progressed largely using Western frameworks and constructions of womanhood. Resultingly, it seems like the fight for different relations between Caribbean men and women is inextricably tied to the United Nations Decade of Women and the middle/intellectual class that organized during that time. Further, feminism became a kind of 'fashion statement' during this decade, It was foisted upon the much older women's movement in the Caribbean as the one and only theoretical and organizational framework that made sense in the pursuit of gender and social justice for Caribbean women.

The fragmented historical account of Caribbean women's efforts to liberate themselves, the cooptation of grassroots women's ideas and dreams by middle class women associated with academy and multilaterals like the United Nations and forced feminist loyalty led to division of women along dualistic bounds – working/middle class women, intelligentsia/'ordinary women', consultants/women with lived experience (Ellis 83–4; Mohammed 23–4). While many writers recognize that feminism has not enjoyed a wide embrace among Caribbean women they still endorse solutions that call for a place of prominence for the ism (Ellis 85). I reject feminism as harmful and embodying white supremacy, patriarchal values and classist inequalities. While I do recognize the usefulness of the work of several writers and organizers who characterize their work as feminist (too numerous to list but inter alia, bell hooks, Audra Lorde, Andaiye and Peggy Antrobus), I interact with these writers as Black, resistance makers and/or champions of queer ways of being. For feminism to be a useful gender and social justice framework, it would have to be reflective and willing to part ways with much of its grounding ideology. I see no usefulness in holding out hope for that. Instead, I lean on womanism – a concept made for us by us and which although I recognize as imperfect, has the conceptual room to be expanded and further shaped.

Alice Walker's now well-repeated assertion that "womanism is to feminism as purple is to lavender" embodies some conflations that I work through in Chapter 3 (19). I think here of a TikTok video[1] I once watched labelled 'the colouring box theory' and which covers the difference between feminism and womanism aptly. The colouring box theory explained why people may be unable to give what another seeks while resisting the unproductive urge to write people off with judgement. A person may have purple, black, white and orange in their repertoire of colours. The colours may align with the emotions of fear, caring, anxiety and anger. Their colouring box differs from that of another who may have blue, lavender, brown and pink representing the emotions of empathy, caring, grief and frustration. To assert that purple and lavender are colours sharing relations oversimplifies the context in which those colours exist and that colours can be embedded within cultural and other meanings that can divide even the most closely related shades. Feminism exists in a completely different colouring box or colour palette than womanism. While womanism fights to hold onto the value that women are not monolithic and gender/gender performances are shaped by other identities such as race or age, feminism thrives on a monolithic construction of womanhood (Williams Ntiri 3–6). Feminism constructs womanhood along patriarchal boundaries with women generally being portrayed as respectable, demure and defenceless. There is no clear sense that feminism has found usefulness for female masculinity, and resultingly, Black womanhood, and other non-conforming ones have given feminists trouble to place. Reified theory may be tidy and palatable for academic tenure tracks but it also occludes the average woman and hinders her from seeing herself reflected in the theory that is to represent her. As a corrective, Layli Phillips, leaning on Alice Walker, reclaims space cut off from the folx – indeed one of the most attractive features of womanism:

> Women's resistance activity [is] squarely within the realm of the "everyday", thereby defying both academic and ideological claims on the definition, labelling, and elaboration of women's resistance activity under the exclusive and limited label "*feminist.*" (xx) (emphasis in the original)

Womanism is a refusal to accept ahistoricity in the CC (or any other places for that matter) that makes the business of creating meaning of women's experiences the domain of middle-class and 'trained' women who carry out 'feminist analysis'. It is accepted that because women like Beatrice and Eulease Hollingsworth could not document their strategies and approaches to womanhood does not mean their approaches and theories were unimportant and valueless. To date, Layli Phillips offers the most comprehensive definition of womanism as theory AND praxis. Though a bit long, I offer it in entirety:

> Womanism is a social change perspective rooted in Black women's and other women of color's everyday experiences and everyday methods of problem solving in everyday spaces, extended to the problem of ending all forms of oppression for all people, restoring balance between people and the environment/nature, and reconciling human life with the spiritual dimension. I take the perspective that womanism is not feminism. Its relationships to feminism (including Black feminism) are important, but its relationships to other critical theories and social-justice movements are equally important, despite being less frequently discussed or acknowledged. Unlike feminism and despite its name, womanism does not emphasize or privilege gender or sexism; rather, it elevates all sites and forms of oppression, whether they are based on social-address categories like gender, race, or class, to a level of equal concern and action. *Womanism's link to gender is the fact that the historically produced race/class/gender matrix that is Black womanhood serves as the origin point for a speaking position that freely and autonomously addresses any topic or problem.* (xx–xxi) (my emphasis added).

I agree wholeheartedly with Phillips that the experience of Black womanhood is an untapped site of possibilities towards a performance of womanhood which overcomes patriarchal and other types of harm. The Caribbean then, as a major site of the creation of Black womanhood, is by no means peripheral but in fact indispensably central.

Claiming space for womanist approaches to meaning-making about Black womanhood requires critical engagement with Western knowledge enterprises. The gains are many, namely alternative space where sisterhood (again) becomes possible beyond segmentation in the CC women's movement. My major methodological approach is a historical, post-oppositional,[2] womanist grounded one. Given the destruction and divisions – perceived or real – caused by CC feminist organizing, I believe it is important to encourage conversations with ourselves and men that challenge the current gender status quo but also leave space for Black women and men to find the solutions together. This book encourages Caribbean women to step back into their history – both of slavery and of their immediate ancestors to find women who had the audacity to define themselves not just as mothers and wives but also as people with the right to create their own parameters and comfort of existence. I contemplate Black women's intimate partnerships with Black men but I resist established gender binaries and norms in reconciling them.

This book but also my community work is intentionally transdisciplinary. I move between queer theory for its value in challenging the gender binary and women's, sexuality and gender studies – naming patriarchy and the gender binary as colonial violence and trauma (Butler xxx–xxxi; Halberstam 126–7; Iantaffi 89–91). The work is historical because reconnecting women's struggles on both sides of the United Nations Decade of Women is an important corrective that unleashes new possibilities in using our past for important and useful patterns of resistance. This history also becomes an important grounding for contemporary possibilities to expand those nascent ways given to us by our progenitors. The connection hopefully gives us the courage to turn our reflections about women's resistance back inward from United Nations and consultant-led accounts to allows us to consider homegrown approaches to womanhood rooted in how grassroots Caribbean women negotiate/d and navigate/d womanhood. There are also perhaps other disciplinary boundaries that I cross in this work because the Caribbean intellectual tradition has always been flexible enough to take account of the fact that knowledge and the making of knowledge should never be broken and compartmentalized to make it easier for the academy to package and label (Henry, *Caliban's Reason* 2–9).

This work aims to contribute to a recalibration of womanhood at a conceptual level – one that celebrates Black women's strength and proximity to masculinity instead of pathologizing or hiding it. Thus, while the period that I draw historical data from is extensive (late 1800s to about 1960), I do not believe this poses significant limitations because I am reading together CC women's in somewhat of a diachronic manner and only for what they teach us about various womanhoods and negotiations of womanhood. My main methods are archival and book research to think through lived experiences of the folx. My return to the Afro-Caribbean archives led me to what I call **two-hand reading.** Two-handed reading is a method of 'history from below'[3] that guards against extending elite practices of social organization, sex and gender performances as the only or the most widely practised choices. Thomas Thistlewood's diaries[4] provide snippets into women's that can be read differently and perhaps beyond his intentions for keeping the diary. Two-hand reading is a method that could operationalize Analouise Keating's threshold theories, which unveil 'new' conceptualizations of the world, in action (Keating 11). The concept of threshold theories can also extend beyond the written and reasoned contributions of women of colour to theories to lived experience of Black people that seek to restore humanity, self-dignity and intellectual pathways to social justice. What Keating does not offer is a way to convert already existing work, that may not be written in a post-oppositional manner, and make it meaningful input to arrive at non-oppositional conclusions. This is important since it is impossible to discard this body of already available work and start afresh. I suggest that two-hand reading can be the mechanism – "a methodological tour de force" in its own right (Nash xv). I did not return to the archives in a primary fashion – that calls for time and financial resources this book project did not have. I used available books about slavery in the Caribbean and North America, largely written without focus on gender relations but which can be reread with a gender lens to illuminate understanding about sex and gender performances during slavery. This method, as it did for me, can reduce the resource overlays necessary to put contemporary and historical (gender) themes in conversation.

Our ancestors gifted us the wisdom that one hand cannot clap. This is especially true when making sense of a region like the Caribbean, or a performance of womanhood like Butch heterosexuality. Focus on any one side of the complex Caribbean matrix will most likely result in misreadings or simplistic postulates. Two-hand reading allows consideration of the admixtures resulting from the Caribbean contact situation, but also just like hands can move different ways to produce different sounds of claps – this type of reading reminds us that there is generative power in mixing. Two-hand reading is engaged. It is an approach to rereading history and available material. It is reading beyond a mechanical process – a book in hand becomes time travel. With pencils, sticky notes and highlighters reading becomes healing. It is not reading to cite a passage or prove a point but pensive and supplicant reading. Two-hand reading refutes binary ways of knowing and understanding the world. Two-hand reading creates enough space for multiple approaches to gender performances, political performances and the wider human existence – to want to explore living in ways that do not demand an outcome of right or wrong. Two-hand reading is important because asking what is necessarily and naturally the other side of the knowledge already available – what is missing for the most complete view possible, encourages makes openness and flexibility. The approach to working through life becomes grappling with what is and not what we dream. Complexity does not become bad or a 'spoke in the wheel'. It is expected and patience and grace to work through complexity becomes a valued life skill. For too long, the reification of knowledge making, separated research outcomes from the world views and life skills used to create them. I think this is a major reason some research work sits on the pages of books irrecoverable to grounding practice. Knowledge reification feeds an absent and disengaged approach to change. Two-hand reading delves for answers to questions that require reflection. It is not just an academic approach but rather it is everyday strategy that can also assist meaning-making in academic endeavour. Two-hand reading is my approach to investigating and outlining butch heterosexuality as a legitimate way that Caribbean women refused the boundaries of Creole society. Moreover, I suggest that it can now be harnessed by those of us women who enjoy sex with men but who refuse to live in relationships of subordination where our mental health, financial well-being and sexual and physical safety are not guaranteed.

Barbados and the CC: Ratoons of Gender

Paget Henry wrote what I think is a brilliant essay that demonstrates how the Caribbean remains peripheral to the world economic system in what he terms the informatic capitalist era. He uses the metaphor of ratooning – an agricultural pruning process used in sugar cane farming – to demonstrate how the CC continues to produce approaches to business that maintain its economic subjugation and failure ("Caribbean Dependence in the Phase of Informatic Capitalism" 172). Having grown up in cane ground and fully understanding the process of ratooning, I think the power of the metaphor applies to more than the economic life of the Caribbean. The decimation of Indigenous populations made the Caribbean a tabula rasa upon which the experience of colonization and more specifically the development of a set of plantation mores and norms resulted in the development of a racial and gendered oppression used to dehumanize Africans trafficked across the Atlantic and forced into chattel slavery. Since the 1600s when the first systems were established, despite whatever adjustments have been made the ratoons continue to emerge – just like sugarcane – across the landscapes of relations between all people, including men and women in the CC. Not even ploughing a ground and changing the crop cultivated stops ratooning. I have seen a field of sweet potatoes with sugar cane that has sprouted up randomly. The only way to diminish gender ratoons is by consciously recognizing how deep seated and embedded the crop is in our ways of knowing and being related to manhood and womanhood. I suggest discarding old approaches and be willing to embrace new formations that are less toxic and more amenable to Black women and men living in harmony. Rewriting gender relations cannot be a passive, soft issue that ruling elites in the Caribbean gloss over. Just like there have been well-planned and orchestrated efforts over time to address and reshape the colonial impacts on Caribbean economy, those impacts must also be named and addressed in conceptions of womanhood specifically and gender relations more broadly. A call for gender reformation in the CC is a call for attention to nuance and dedication to fix relations between Black men and Black women. It is a commitment to anti-patriarchal approaches to partnering. I agree with Orlando Patterson's guidance that it is useful not to simply lump all of the Caribbean's slave past together when discussing social phenomenon or to use data from one specific period alone to generalize (Patterson xv; xvii–xviii). I suggest that the material and periods covered in this book occur as three ratoons. There are those from 1600s to legal emancipation, legal emancipation to the 1930s Uprisings and the 1930s to Independence. Understanding the themes and features of these periods can elucidate the contemporary treatment of womanhood in Barbados. What is really responsible for the gender war in Barbados, if there is indeed one, is laid bare and that allows space to reconceptualize what a different future could be.

1600 – Legal Emancipation first Ratooning

During the 1600s there was a rapid establishment of colonies across the Caribbean. By 1616, Raymond Smith notes that the first plantation had been established in Bermuda (8). Large-scale agriculture started in Barbados in 1627 while in Jamaica by 1655 the English were establishing foothold on settlement. While the stories of settlement in each of the territories of the CC reveal different demographic factors, one of the underlining theme of importance and present everywhere was the level of brutality and human suffering needed to create plantation societies. This brutality is key when considering the formation of gender values and performances in the contemporary Caribbean. As Orlando Patterson explains, might in plantation societies replaced the social compact underpinning cohesion in other settlements (xli). Reading dominion and dulotic scholarship about the forced Atlantic crossings of Africans; experiences of Black people living under slavery (in the Caribbean but also the United States), glimpses of the tensions that emerge in plantation gender relations are possible.

The brutality of Black women and men started during the capture in Africa. Saidiya Hartman in *Lose Your Mother: A Journey Along the Atlantic Slave Route* documents a girl who had boarded a trafficking vessel with venereal disease (140). Sailors' crews on trafficking vessels enjoyed liberal access to sex from the women and girls they trafficked as a 'perk' of their jobs (141). Hilary Beckles portrays the treatment of women and girls on slave ships as a part of the 'seasoning' that made them submit to life in Barbados (*Natural Rebels* 27). Throughout the experience of capture both in Africa and on plantations, Black women were subjected to rape and sexual abuse to appease the curiosities of white men but also as a part of the terror and used to assert white manhood as the dominant one (Beckles, "Perfect Property" 149–50; Patterson xviii). Edward Baptist documents the connections between promiscuity, prospecting and business in the entire economic enterprise associated with slavery in the United States (233–41). Hilary Beckles notes the importance of sex as a commodity in the economics of Barbados (*Natural Rebels* 141–4).

Black men were forced to spectate the brutality meted out to Black, and being rendered helpless to save their lovers, daughters, mothers was one of the ways that the Black man was infantilized and emotionally bruised. Trying to come to the rescue of the Black female was an infraction punishable by Black male death (Foster, *Rethinking Rufus* 32–3; Patterson 42). The realities faced by Black men and women resulted in specific gender performances. Black men, for self-preservation, did not practice protection of female kin. Black women were responsible for themselves and their children as best they could. Black women were not keen to bring children into the torture of slavery and abortion and contraception were widely practised (Beckles, *Natural Rebels* 97; Patterson 106–9). Patterson also notes that some women delayed or refused motherhood altogether because it spoiled their desirability to men in a society where providing sexual services was legitimate and profitable business. Since hard work was rewarded with some level of 'privilege' both men and women were motivated by work. There was no value to Black women of being 'delicate' or 'soft' (Beckles, *Natural Rebels* 24). In other words, from very early in the slave enterprise in the Caribbean, Black women in plantation societies exhibited elements of strength, working outside and being independent, usually traits marked as masculine.

Orlando Patterson and Hilary Beckles assert that enslaved Africans practised 'polygamy' and they present this as an African retention (Patterson 107; Beckles, *Natural Rebels* 117). Although both Beckles and Patterson accept that multi-partnering was a feature of plantation society from very early on, they both present polygamy as if it is a male gender performance only. Patterson does not use the word 'polygamy' to describe Black women's refusal to marry and to have multiple partners (Black and white). I have rejected Beckles' assertion that polygamy is an African retention because it is oversimplified and reductionist (Hinds Myrie 7–9). Further, even if one wants to label what occurred in the first stage of plantation society as polygamy, Walter Rodney classifies it as a system that was exploitative of women (274). Applying two-handed reading to the situation in early slave society could reveal that rather than multi-partnering being an African retention it could also have been gender and sexuality performances of Black men and Black women resulting from geographical/social interruption and insertion/influence of colonial practice in CC plantations. In other words, gender relations changed to suit plantation society. As Burnard and Garrigus explain, plantation societies were "… new and disturbing places where traditional gender roles came under considerable stress and sometimes alteration" (76). Multi-partnering and transactional sex were two features of plantation sexuality in both male and female life – Black and white. It must be noted that marriage was an exception and not a norm in all aspects of plantation life (Burnard 67–71; Patterson 41–2). In the face of rampant and widespread rape and debauchery, Black women learnt how to present themselves as strong and self-contained. They developed a performance of femininity that suited the social construction of them which Hilary Beckles describes:

> The black woman, then was conceptually defeminized and desexualized within pro-slavery discourse in ways that exposed her to the violent sexuality of white males for whom she was primarily a form of property. The creation of a social world that attached nothing positive in terms of human value to the black skin kept her prisoner as a life-server; furthermore, it eroded important aspects of her sense of beauty and inner worth. Because she was unable to socially legitimate her beauty within the dominant culture, the "black and ugly" narrative had a telling effect upon her decision making and ultimately shaped much of the aesthetic of the black community. Resistance to this colour representation was,

> however, relentless. *A counter-aesthetic emerged as a site of resistance that was as important as the battlefields of violent self-liberation (*my emphasis*)* ("Perfect Property" 153).

I suggest that masculine femininity is a part of the counter-aesthetic and gender performances of womanhood to choose from in Black women's liberatory struggle during slavery. Even though defeminization and desexualization may have begun as states enacted on Black women, they became states that Black women exploited for their agency. Masculine femininity was practised by Black women on the plantation because it was useful. Rather than seeing masculine femininity as a pathology to be hidden or fixed, it has been a survival mechanism harnessed by our foremothers for its usefulness. What I am contending here, is that by the time the period of Emancipation gender relations become impacted by Victorian beliefs, but there is also a ratoon of gender norms from an earlier era. Black women maintained practices because there were still relevant and useful in the context of plantation society.

Legal Emancipation to 1930s Uprisings second Ratooning

While the germination and practice of the gender performance that I call butch heterosexuality finds it roots in the earliest formations of plantation society, it is during the Victorian era (1837–1901) that it comes under the most scrutiny in plantation societies. This period coincided with the legal emancipation of kidnapped Africans and Britain's quest to 'purify' family relations. Institutions were opened in England to remove women involved in prostitution from the streets (Wilson 141). Homosexual coupling was also targeted as inappropriate (190–1), (Iantaffi 23–4). The attacks on expansive gender performance happened because Victorian era values legitimated the gender binary upon which contemporary patriarchy rests. Womanhood functionally clearly delineated masculinity as only belonging to males. Good femininity deferred to masculinity and helped to enforce its primacy. Judith Butler describes the constitutive relationship (Victorian) between masculinities and femininities as "compulsory heterosexuality" (xxx).

At the time of legal emancipation in Barbados and the CC, there was not much incentive for women to relinquish the strength and self-reliance that had protected them in earlier years of plantation society. The economic situation across the CC meant that women still had to work because their male partners were unable to provide for them financially. Additionally Rhoda Reddock's important research contextualizes the fact that features of the sexual distribution of labour are not universal. In other words, while every society will have some division of tasks between women and men, what is seen as women's work and men's work is context dependent (Reddock, *Women Labour and Politics in Trinidad and Tobago* 2–3). Caribbean women have always worked outside of the home, I argue in ways that have shaped their performances of womanhood. Black women were not seen as needing protection or support. While that fact was responsible for much of the brutality Black women faced during the plantation enterprise, it was also a source of autonomy. It is instructive that during a murderous, late-night plot in eighteenth-century Barbados, the boy sent out to do the deed dressed as a woman (Fuentes 50–1). Black women's movement was relatively 'free' and not restricted in ways that women with 'virtue' were. These notions of freedom and movement were transferred to the post-emancipation period.

Both women and men opted for family unions where conjugal partners visited each other much in the same way as what is being called 'living together apart' in post-COVID Canada. Although Hilary Beckles reads the performance of polygamy as a male behaviour (*Natural Rebels* 118–19) being separate from partners gave Caribbean women as much freedom to have multiple partners as it did men (Chevannes 131; Mohammed and Perkins 72). This practice was especially important in maintaining economic freedom. Coupling separation meant women could carry on relationships with plantation overseers and other resource holders during slavery and after without losing autonomy and sexual freedom. Women formed as many strategic alliances as they could to support them and their children. Thus, despite focused efforts to get Caribbean women and men to invest in and practice legal marriage, there was little interest either side (Moore 113–17). Barry Chevannes explains that where common law or visiting relationships were once marked undesirable class marker, the practice gained legitimacy in Jamaica and across the CC because it is being practised widely (as well as outside the Caribbean as noted above) (190–1). Although emancipation generally failed to be widespread liberation for Black descendants of stolen Africans, there were minute legal changes that signalled gains in women's autonomy over their bodies. For instance, rape of a Black woman – which was formerly not a crime became so across the CC from 1826 in Barbados, Jamaica and other territories under British rule. The point cannot be overstated because law and social change are usually not seamless, and Beckles notes that the fines associated with rape were menial and cases hard to prove (*Natural Rebels* 42). Black women's power and agency incrementally increased and with the advent of Black power and nationalistic movements their confidence and validity in themselves increased.

Women have always been active partners in liberation struggles in the Caribbean. Accounts about women's resistance struggles in the Caribbean appear in the work of Verene Shepherd, Rhoda Reddock, Lucille Mathurin-Mair and Hilary Beckles, to name a few. During the 1930s uprisings they joined forces to agitate for change in the plantation social order and for greater access to amenities like food housing and decent work. Rhoda Reddock's *Women, Labour and Politics in Trinidad and Tobago* provides an important account of how women began to organize themselves both in pursuit of Black liberation and also their own liberation between the 1930s and Independence in the 1960s. In chapters six and nine, Reddock examines the contribution of Audrey Jeffers, whose is described as both nationalist and feminist (*Women Labour and Politics in Trinidad and Tobago* 166). Jeffers advocacy navigates equal work for equal pay issues (*Women Labour and Politics in Trinidad and Tobago* 165); participation in politics (*Women Labour and Politics in Trinidad and Tobago* 174–5); and voting and encouraging women to vote (*Women Labour and Politics in Trinidad and Tobago* 242–5). Jeffers organized with notable nationalists and trade unionists including A. A. Cipriani. CC women's liberation struggles have always fermented at the intersection of gender and race. It is one of the reasons that Caribbean women had ideological contentions with feminism.

1930s Uprisings to Independence third Ratooning

The contributions of women outlined by Reddock in the 1930s Caribbean are similar to those outlined by Jill Hamilton for Barbados. Like their Trinidad and Tobago sisters, Barbadian women used the cause of the indigent and suffering to organize themselves and offer assistance (44). Hamilton also traces the development of schools catering to girls from as early as 1824 (42). Notwithstanding that school would have been a limited privilege, it means that there were models of the value and freedom education afforded in the imagination of Barbadian women. As the years went by and more schools opened across Barbados, 'a proper education' was valued for both boys and girls. In my own family, children were educated not according to gender but to who the parents thought would 'take in the learning' better. Caribbean women, who had always worked outside the home found employment in new industries including garment making and tourism. Despite women's willingness to work, they have been hampered by the problem of unemployment which is a feature of dependency economies (Givan xx–xxi; Mohammed and Perkins 35). The lack of employment restricted some women and forced them to remain in relationships characterized by unequal power relations.

Two-hand reading explicates the complexity of gender relations in post-1930s Barbados and the CC. Notwithstanding the gains that women made, they were also not fully integrated into their new societies. Although the history of slavery clearly shows that CC Black women have never performed a femininity that was helpless, supple and pliable, Black men contemplating freedom wanted the patriarchal dream. After subjugated and disrespected during slavery, Black men in the Caribbean were ready to be free but their models of freedom were the white patriarchs who exploited and looted the region under plantation. Many of those white men had dominion over no one else but their Black kidnapped and enslaved African 'property'. To be free, Black men in the Caribbean wanted that same power and dominion over Black women and subordinate women as white men had enjoyed. With no more access to land or economic liberation than they had under the system of slavery, what else could Black Caribbean men control but 'their women'? (Beckles, *A History of Barbados* 208–9; Cummins 80–1; Thomas, *Exceptional Violence* 82–4). The need to control something to exercise manhood has resulted in tense and acrimonious gender relations on the Caribbean heterosexual scene. Lucille Mathurin-Lair captures some of the complexity well in the article "Reluctant Matriarchs". Mathurin-Mair contends that while there is pervading "myth of the black matriarch, the mother-who-fathered countless generations of West Indians, and who in the process demoralised and feminised husband, lover, brother and son" the reality is that the "economically depressed condition of such a female breadwinner makes her sexually vulnerable as she was in the darker days of her history" (130 and 133). Every action that Caribbean woman takes to liberate themselves is construed as a direct and deliberate threat to men. Moreover, it was during the post-1930s ratooning that feminist organizing became prominent. Rather than a historically continuous reading of Caribbean women's performances of womanhood, many blamed feminisms for the ways that Caribbean women were resisting patriarchy in newly independent territories.

A read of daily newspapers in Barbados and their comments sections will reveal that there is a general view that feminism has caused women to rise up resulting in the subjugation of men and destruction of the family. In offering Butch heterosexuality as a type of performance of femininity, I suggest that slavery and its institutions destroyed the Black family and women used their resilience to cope as best they could. Caribbean women today are no more 'controllable' perhaps than our foremothers were and maybe the magic of better relations between Caribbean men and women is for men to understand their history and their women – not through the falsehoods of Victorian womanhood and patriarchy, but reality. Obviously, there is a large period of time between the independence movement and the contemporary moment in the Caribbean. I believe that the same features of the third ratooning repeat themselves in this period. So although it is a long time span the changes to gender relations have stagnated and recycled. I hope that this conceptual offering contributes to other possibilities for understanding Caribbean women, their performances of womanhood and a new set of relations that can better serve women, men and the families they build together.

The Chapters

Chapter 1, The Creation of Plantation, sets out the plantation as cite of unequal power relations and oppressive structures. These power relations underpin all aspects of business and life and became solidified as social constructs related to the process of colonialization and creating settler and plantation societies. Gender is socially constructed, and the chapter demonstrates how the social constructs of plantation affected the citizenship experience of individual categories of people in the plantation society. While some writers have taken up the social construction of gender/race/sex/class relations, in terms of how Black and mulatto women used sex as currency to buy freedom or at least reprieve from the hardest labour, this chapter considers how women created a masculine performance of womanhood which I contend were another approach women activated to cope with the atrocities of plantation. This chapter outlines the ratoons of female masculinities and sets it up as a possibility to be applied to the vagaries of other periods in history including legal emancipation, independence and post-independence.

Chapter 2, Breaking Silence: State/Family Dysfunction and Plantation, traces the continued logics of plantation and how they move from characterizing white individualist patriarchy to Black manhood and state creation in the nationalist period. Errol Miller's marginalization theory is used as an example of the views that Black Caribbean men held and still hold about Black women. These views affect policy positions and intimate relations. The extent of freedom of the social self is the extent of freedom of the individual self. The chapter reveals that Black women still live in a present absence in their societies and families. A two-handed reading of the abolition of the Bastardry laws reveals that motherhood in the Caribbean is a mechanism of control manipulated to maintain plantation status quo and PPC. Rather than seeing the national culture as separate from what pertains in the family, it is read as a continuum where the national culture legitimate family violence and instability through mechanisms like the family court. The chapter ends with a case study of a Barbadian woman, Maude that combines the themes across the micro (family) level to the macro (nationalist) level to show contemporary issues in Caribbean womanhood and the response to family violence and instability.

Chapter 3, Butch Heterosexuality: Black Women Are (Gender) Innovators, argues that fixing CC gender relations is a decolonial project. It requires changes in nationalist goals and integration of the populations cut off from their full citizenship rights by plantation values, including women, disabled, queer individuals and children. The meaning of freedom and nationalist society must change to facilitate a change in gender relations between men and women at the state level. Trauma-informed approaches to intimate partner relations can dismantle harmful and engrained PPC and its relationship dynamics between Black men and Black women. Butch heterosexuality creates space for this gender reconfiguration by making performances of womanhood that do not facilitate patriarchal relations the only ones and Black men aware and accepting of that. I work through a definition of womanism that can replace feminism as a major organizational tool for women in the CC, including women who are outside of the expected 'respectable' performances of womanhood.

Chapter 4, Redefining Heterosexual Partnership: Building Anti-Patriarchal Relationships by Prioritizing Healing puts the key themes of all the chapters in conversation. Plantation depends on a 'double consciousness' where there are open secrets that no one speaks. This chapter concludes this book by breaking all silence around Butch heterosexuality. Theoretical ends are tied up through the work of Judith Butler and Jack Halberstam. Black men and women taking responsibility for their individual healing thereby showing up for healthy partnership and delinking from harmful colonial, white notions of femininity and masculinity are some of the suggestions about how the dynamics of opposite sex partnering can be challenged and changed.

Notes

1 We should be mindful that social media makes information available and simultaneously easily lost. I spent many hours searing to recover the video to cite in this book and was unable to find it.

2 Analouise Keaton contends that Western scholarship and approaches to knowledge making produce flawed oppositional toolkits that cannot bring about the urgent transformations we need in dealing with some of the most significant, contemporary, existential threats. She explains that, oppositional thinking "inhibit[s] our ability to develop and implement innovative strategies for progressive social change" (8).

3 Mimi Sheller's definition of thinking about social experiences from the 'below' is well set out and cogent (24–6).

4 I use Douglas Hall's *In Miserable Slavery* and Trevor Burnard's *Mastery, Tyranny and Desire* to access the diaries.

1 The Creation of Plantation

Barbados severed with the British monarchy in 2021. The rhetoric associated with the change was that the termination and a Barbadian head of state completed the independence project. Notwithstanding, simultaneous with the hype and excitement about the change, the entire Island was engulfed in a debate about the atrocities confronting girls who were deprived of their freedom and incarcerated in the Government Industrial School.[1] The girls, mainly children in need of care due to childhood sexual abuse, family instability or mental wellness/illness challenges, were being detained under an archaic law called wandering. Originally, the wandering law was designed to punish Black people who refused to stay on or work for plantation after legal emancipation. Even as Barbados boasted the completion of its project of independence through declaring itself a republic without a British monarchical head of state the available logics and through processes underpinning policies to treat one of the most vulnerable sector of Barbadians were steeped in harmful gender norms and misogyny. Girls, both those at the Government Industrial School and those who are affected by adverse gender logics in almost every aspect of their lives, are an example of George Beckford's assertion that, "the modern Caribbean society displays structural forms that are a direct legacy of the slave plantation system. The legacy provides the single most important clue for an understanding of contemporary Caribbean society" (109).

The plantation is far more than the crop grown in large production formation and to understand that is to grasp how, despite a change in legal status of independence or republic, Barbados is still at its core, a plantation. Plantation as a system of social relations refers to the psycho/socio/political characteristics that result in a country being organized based on hierarchy and subordination for the economic and emotional gain of a small minority. The status quo at the top of the plantation hierarchy – historically cis white men – have been supplanted by a politourgeoisie. I depend on Gramsci's theory of cultural hegemony in defining politourgeoisie. In Gramsci's model the bourgeoisie employ tactics of social and intellectual superiority to separate themselves from the masses and preserve their unfair advantages in business and society (Gramsci 8–9). The **po'litour'geoisie** is a special

DOI: 10.4324/9781003518709-2

kind of bourgeoisie that arises largely out of the same subjugation and non-access to financial resources as the majority of the Black population in Barbados and the Caribbean. Some members of the politourgeoisie may be descendants of Black professionals who, through professional and other connections rose further in society than others. Since the politourgeoisie is seen as having done well in education or professions, this grants them access to progressive systems in Commonwealth Caribbean (CC) society such as political and labour organizations. It is at this point that rather than using their power and position to assist other members of the dispossessed class from which they emerge, the politourgeoisie hegemonize their other types of privileges – family connections, school tie connections and memberships in elite clubs, lodges and churches – to disassociate from the masses and then manipulate the rest of the society mainly driven by their access to governmental political power. Where bourgeoisie may depend on generational heritage of money and status, politourgeoisie rely heavily on delusion, veneer, and trickery to maintain their social position – the emperors really have no clothes. The politourgeoisie and the way that they function is a decidedly colonial relic and one that is not just a feature of Caribbean society. Chika Oneyeani outlines the phenomenon copiously in Africa:

> The lack of commitment to the real meaning of freedom and independence by those African leaders who "won" independence for their respective countries form their former colonial masters has done more to impugn the intelligence of the Blackman and raise more questions about his ability to govern himself. Today Africa is worse off than when it gained independence from the colonial masters. The standard of living of the masses has decreased steadily…there is more malnutrition, more disease, less provision of essential services…and less freedom to express one's views. …Africa has incurred more debt, yet has nothing to show for it. The debts incurred were used more for grandiose projects than for services for the people.
>
> [Africa's elite is] intellectual[ly] bankrupt. [They] stand out as the single group which has damaged Africa most because of their quest for an easy life of luxury. This is the group that took on the baton form the former colonial rulers. They took on the opulent life lived by the oppressor. Rather than eliminate the excesses of the Caucasian masters, the elite saw their takeover as an opportunity to double the pain of the masses of the people. Their claim to the throne vacated by the Caucasian was that they had gone to school, an education in which partial learning was not a requirement. The elite inherited the European position.
>
> The Europeans … decided to let [the African elite] be perceived as having taken over, and they exercised, and continue to exercise, power over [the African elite] in any major decision making. (98–100)

This chapter reengaged the literature available on the slavery enterprise for early gender clues, especially the ones that show African women resisting their subjugation. I want to pay attention to the brutality visited on everyone who was associated with plantation and set out some of the major hierarchical divisions in plantation society according to racial and gender identities. This chapter shows clearly that Beckford's assertion about plantation as a social system is important in understanding Caribbean history but also contemporary formations.

White Men and Plantation

> Monday 22nd [July 1765]: Last night J[ohn] H[artnole] having overeat himself in the Savanna, shit in the great house. (D. Hall 137)

The freest that any man could be in the seventeenth and eighteenth centuries was to be a white man connected to the enterprise of Transatlantic slavery, white men in the Caribbean were free of bowels, deprived of the guiding principles of humanity and full of clap! White male freedom in the Caribbean rose exponentially with was 'slave' owning. Douglas Hall[2] and Trevor Burnard[3] show the excesses, riches and brutality of white men in Caribbean society using the diaries of Thomas Thistlewood. Thistlewood was a common-born second son of an English farmer. After being unsuccessful trying to establish himself in England, Thistlewood decided to seek employment in a colony. The decision ended up being one that allowed him to become a well-established and 'respected' man in Jamaica and to make more money than he ever would had he stayed in England (T. Burnard 15). Dehumanization of Black people forced into slavery in the Caribbean benefitted white men the most. As Burnard explains, white men living in plantation society had both their sexual and emotional needs provided by Black women (67). It was in this context that white men were allowed to experience a satisfying patriarchy because in many cases they never presided over white women in the same way either at home or in the colonies.

Plantocratic Patriarchal Culture

Gerda Lerner, in her diachronic study of the development of patriarchy, explains that women forfeited autonomy for protection given the structure of hunter-gatherer societies (Lerner 52–3). 1492 and the development of Transatlantic slavery saw another dimension added to the playbook of patriarchy. The traditional features of patriarchy – hierarchical social formation, men's control of women's reproductive, emotional and manual labour – remained. Added to it was racial subjugation and a concentrated level of dehumanization and deprivation of autonomy for classes of people – Black and Indigenous. Where patriarchy had been predicated on the spoils of war, and enslavement in its earliest periods much like it was in the CC, traditional patriarchy was still somewhat 'kept in check' by it being based on the needs of the communal or community. 1492 gave rise to individualistic patriarchy set down solely on accumulation and money but without a service or loyalty to communal or community. There were no restrictions on a patriarch and his ego and satisfying it the only guide (Dunn 337–8). The emergent society and culture is plantocratic patriarchal culture (PPC). PPC is the petri dish of individualistic patriarchy and the one that enables the other – "PPC is a system of racial/ social hierarchies and unchecked patriarchal rights and privileges. Subjugation of women – and other groups of 'undeserving citizens' is germinal to PPC and without unequal relations, PPC cannot survive" (Hinds Myrie 2).

Along with their unfettered access to sex, white men in the Caribbean ensured they had unfettered access in the political and judicial domains. The courts in the Caribbean were not set up as annals of justice but rather an important legal institution in the construction of white male power and control. The judicial system legitimated the unequal social relations of plantation. An element of the dehumanization of Black people in the Caribbean was their lack of access to justice or rights before the court (Nash xvii). While it was almost impossible for an enslaved African to sue someone, the law was stacked against any Black person accused of harming a white person (Patterson 85). Plantation judiciary upheld the unchecked power of white male dominance but concomitantly, Kamau Brathwaite clearly articulates using the example of the American War that, Caribbean colonists did not want true freedom. They were content to make their riches connected to the economy of England and its preferential prices (Brathwaite 68–73). The white planters in the Caribbean had become lazy in their business thinking and heavily dependent on their preferentially rigged system. Brathwaite reads this as causing the demise of the colony of Jamaica (94). It was profit and high living that concerned the planters and work was seen as a necessary evil best avoided if at all possible (Dunn 6).

The plantation political system had a poorly functioning approach to governance and patronage/paternalism was a significant aspect of the system (Patterson 31–2; T. Burnard 78). Paternalism/patronage is used as a mechanism of individualistic patriarchy. Status positions such as Thoman Thistlewood's military commission were important because they brought prestige and respectability to individualist ego (D. Hall 221–2). Positions of responsibility and government power, often gained through personal friendships and other social connections, legitimated individualist patriarchs in plantocratic patriarchal societies. White patriarchs held not much more interests in the position than what they could procure for individual gain. An example of this is when Thistlewood considers procuring a red military jacket, which had no real use outside of pomp and which he decides against due to the financial outlay it would have required (D. Hall 118–19). This political system remains in the Caribbean and works in specific ways to uphold a dominant masculinity to the detriment of Caribbean women and girls and other groups in society. This discussion continues in Chapter Two. It is true that white men had and created for themselves in the Caribbean absolute and unchallenged power. The society in which they lived was characteristically patriarchal even though both Black and white women resisted the hegemony.

Effect of PPC on Marriage

Marriages up until the eighteenth century were fraught. Many challenges afflicted marriage, including high-death rates, low interest from both white women and white men to be married and white men's preferences to force themselves on enslaved Black women due to unequal rights/power relations, fetishization and ease (T. Burnard 67–71; Baptist 241; Moore 113). Thomas Thistlewood was turned down for marriage to a white woman before he left England. In the Caribbean, dominion over land and 'slaves' (both male and female) gave him another route to patriarchal domination and thus he never sought white marriage again (T. Burnard 38). In addition to the general challenges that undermined marriage, in plantation societies, white men's further departure from the family as a patriarchal base unit had severe effects on white women's marriage possibilities (see section on White Women below). Thistlewood, like so many white men in the plantation society, depended on "slave women (SIC), [like] his mistress Phibbah, [to] satisfy[y] his sexual and **emotional needs**" (T. Burnard 67). I believe that it is worth underlining the emotional labour carried out by Black women for white men during slavery in the Caribbean. While relationships such as the one Thistlewood had with Phibbah were grounded in unequal sexual power relations, two-handed reading is important to understanding the complexity and possibility in the encounters. For many white men like Thistle who remained unmarried, their relationships with Black and mulatto[4] women were their primary liaisons. Their Black and mulatto women, through pillow talk offered advice about business, and suggestions about making house home – all the activities associated with 'wifehood' (and much like women do now). Thomas Thistlewood made a clear differentiation between transactional sex, which from his time in England he rewarded with payment and the more personal relationship he built with Phibbah. She was integrated into his business dealings. On several occasions Phibbah lent Thistlewood money (D. Hall 94; 143). The white woman from whom Thistlewood brought his property was a close friend of Phibbah's and it is not a stretch to believe that Phibbah helped Thistlewood broker the deal given the extent of her involvement in his trading business and their exchanges of money and product.[5] The hatred white women felt for Black women on plantation and which shows up today in the strangest places, including inside feminist thought and exclusion, is a direct result of them being rendered useless by the movement of white men from paternal and fraternal patriarchy to individualistic patriarchy[6] in plantation societies. That Black and mulatto women who held the role of mistress to white men were influencers and decision makers in their engagements with white men is an important point to bear in mind in understanding the development of what I call Butch heterosexuality. At their weakest and most dispossessed Black women were still valued for their ability to shoulder the emotional burden of others. They were always resourceful and found ways to survive in the brutality and vagary of plantation. Black women were the ones who developed provision grounds that were valuable to bolstering the food supply of the plantation workforce (Beckles, *Natural Rebels* 77–9). These grounds were also used by Black women (and (their) men) as a source of product that was exchanged or sold to support themselves from starvation on plantation. Why then would they move away from their agency during the Emancipation and Independence eras instead of cultivate it further?

White women had more of a vested interest in supporting the idea of Victorian marriage as a part of Enlightenment values in plantation society than Black women. It gave them hope to regain place and position in individualistic patriarchy. The white women did not necessarily mind white men keeping patriarchal views, they wanted legitimation and space in those views. There is a paradox in the thinking and one that lives on in the contemporary moment especially in feminism through respectability politics. If men are the problem – pass laws and create social norms to policewomen. This tactic plays itself out time and again for example blaming women's dress for sexual assault and the centuries long struggle over bodily autonomy and abortion. Victorian marriage was thought to be solution to controlling the excesses of individualistic patriarchy as it has developed in plantation society. Black women's sexuality and choices were shamed and blamed for white men's willingness to choose Black women. Black women were chosen because they were easy prey – socially vulnerable due to the lack of laws that protected them and limited their financial options. When white men in PPC refused to give up their unabandoned reign by embracing marriage and Black women were blamed for it.

If it can be conceived of any kind of 'love' that guided the actions of white men towards their Black sex slaves, it was 'love' subjugated by white supremacy – love as manipulation. Notwithstanding the importance of Black and mulatto women to white men in plantation societies, white men understood and knew that the division between white/free and Black/unfree had to be maintained at every cost. Love had to be subjugated when the object of love stood to threaten the social order that enabled white men to be all powerful. Love and/or jealousy in relations between white men and Black women fed tensions in white society. William Crookshanks and Thistlewood's relations soured over disagreements their respective mistresses had (T. Burnard 98; 99). This disagreement could have threatened the Egypt plantation where the two men worked. Whereas Crookshanks did not understand the necessity to maintain white rights regardless of what happened, Thistlewood did and the outcome of the two men's fortunes was directly related to their decision. Crookshanks goes against white supremacy and died in ruins, while Thistlewood maintains the status quo and went on to become a 'gentleman' (T. Burnard 98; 99).

'Gentlemen' in Barbados and the CC during colonial rule (and still) could exact their sexual will over any enslaved African with impunity. Sex was an important part of plantation life – it satisfies fetishes; is a tool of terror and subjugation and since the Black womb was where human becomes slave, it was also a means of replenishing workforce. When Thistlewood came to Jamaica in 1750 he brought with him a collection of risque books (T. Burnard 107). Notably his punishment of slaves up to about 1756 revealed a sadistic flair (D. Hall 71–3). Sexual predation, lack of restraint and free reign to work through fetishes were a part of the dominant hegemonic masculinity associated with plantation society in the CC. Where Thistlewood may have been judged or found it difficult to negotiate his fetishes with bodily excretion, sex and punishment in English society or American colony, he is free to experiment with the bodies of his Caribbean slaves. Douglas Hall cautiously surmises that Thistlewood's behaviour may have changed due to his relationship with Phibbah – a Black woman (Black not mulatto). This is a guardedly plausible explanation because Thistlewood's diary does reveal Phibbah exercising a modicum of agency. When she and Thistlewood disagreed, Phibbah refused to join him in bed at night (67). It could also be that Thistlewood acted out his fetishes and moved on to new and other conquers. Even at the height of the free reign of white dominant hegemonic masculinity, Black women were not simply prostrate. Black women were not seen as deserving of protection in the same way that white women were but this also resulted in more "freedom" for Black women. They moved at night (D. Hall 76). They also conducted relationships that were beneficial to them with both white and Black men. There is no need to overstate the freedom of Black women during slavery. All I am suggesting is that there was a nascent set of gender norms in plantations society that saw Black women valued for their ability to survive and to provide emotional labour, business advice and perhaps even – as in the case of Phibbah and Thistlewood – to put the guard rails on conscience that stopped dominant patriarchs from descending into total depravity and dehumanization.

Black Men and Plantation

It is no doubt that slavery affected the Black woman in a matrix of gendered and racialized, complicated ways. To accept that is by no means to diminish that slavery also had significant racialized and psychological impacts on Black men. Thomas Foster, through his exploration of Black men's experience of slavery even elucidates some ways that slavery affected Black men in gendered and sexualized ways. Black men were both victimized and brutalized by the back breaking work associated with slavery and they victimized those closest to them – each other and their women and children during Transatlantic slavery.

Much like women developed different performances of womanhood to manage PPC and plantation, likewise men obviously did. As in the case of Black women, many of the performances have led to stereotypes of Black masculinity and research and writing from the perspective of critical/conscious Black researchers is important and necessary in unravelling Black Caribbean masculinities. There is a significant gap in the research about slavery in Barbados and the CC that traces the psychological effects of slavery. For instance, Hilary Beckles writes extensively about Barbados and its ability to 'naturally' reproduce its slave population. While readers get an account of this from a demographic perspective the only thing Beckles is willing to say about its effects on manhood is that Barbadian men are polygamous. Beckles does not so much highlight the fact that the 'natural increase' in Barbados is a system of forced breeding – a system that Thomas Foster's views as psychological and sexualized violence. Beckles in his own explanation of the mechanics of the system clearly alludes to the fact that breeding was incentivized and coerced by white masters. His chapter, "Breeding Wenches" documents the practices of dehumanizing and forced reproduction for women but he addresses the corollary for men as though it is a complete act of male agency (*Natural Rebels* 97). Beckles conflates the implications of the forced coupling and reproduction with 'naturalness' and relationships among African and African descended people in Barbados, especially when he is analysing male behaviour.

This is a common practice in discussing masculine behaviour in slave discourses in the CC context. It disconnects Barbadian and Caribbean men from the scholarship that has been done to highlight the emotional and psychological impacts of forced sexual coupling on the Black community. Of some of the major effects on men of forced breeding, Thomas Foster writes, "forced reproduction divided men along lines of fertility and virility, isolated men who were prolific, and fractured families and communities. Forcing men to father children was but one way that slavery affected gender and sexuality for enslaved men" (*Rethinking Rufus* 46). The afterlives of this forced reproduction are still with us in the contemporary Caribbean. Caribbean men are still comfortable to make children and remove themselves from them financially and emotionally. Although many Black men desire to rule over someone – usually a Black woman and to complete that rule they expect Black women to be supple, agreeable and sexually available they refuse the responsibility that come with fatherhood. Any hint of another kind of femininity is seen as a direct affront to Black men. They will eschew emotional bonds with children but also use children as an ultimate kind of control over the lives of women. Although this male behaviour is a harmful colonial relic there is not a concerted focus on changing it.

Black Men and Individualistic Patriarchy

Individualistic patriarchy was not created by or for Black men because that would have been a direct threat to white supremacy and male dominance. For individualist white patriarchs to be supreme Black men had to be subjugated and exploited. Individualistic patriarchy undermined Black masculinity. It diminished the viability of marriage, for example, and Black men's ability to care for and protect their families. Thistlewood's diaries reveal that he continued to sleep with women who he knew were wives of stolen male Africans (D. Hall 121; 155; 184). White men could physically or sexually take Black women at any point in time as a part of their psychological torture of Black men (Foster, *Rethinking Rufus* 32; 34). Individualistic patriarchy created a paradox for Black men with significant negative consequences for them, the Black family and Black community well-being. While at the root of individualist patriarchy is a diminution and dismissal of Black masculinity, it is also the system of dominant masculinity that became desirable and widespread in Barbados and the CC. Trevor Burnard reads Thomas Thistlewood's garden as a "repository of Enlightenment intellectual energy" (T. Burnard 126). This assertion underlines the fact that the Enlightenment holds Black men and women in non-human positionality. Black men were subjected to psychological and physical terror to elevate white individualistic patriarchs into prominence. Burnard believes that Thistlewood had a particular appreciation for Lincoln his stolen African because he was the first to elevate Thistlewood to a slave owner (T. Burnard 197).

At every turn, PPC diminished the autonomy and emotional wellness of Black men to the benefit of white men and their system. Although the system of individualistic patriarchy succeeded by the subjugation and dehumanization of Black men they aspired to the dominant masculinity they saw performed around them. This desire by Black men is an example of the paradoxes of plantation or as Frantz Fanon metaphorizes, the contradictory masks. White men allowed them Black men measure of autonomy but that autonomy was seasoned with manipulation. When Thistlewood's nephew strikes up a relationship with Little Mimber who is paired with slave driver Johnnie, Thistlewood was not approving. On the face of it, it seems a case of Thistlewood defending Johnnie's honour. However, given the fact that Thistlewood continues his own sexual relationship with Mimber and several other women who were matched to Black men it is reasonable to conclude it was probably more a case of Thistlewood defending his right to Mimber's sexuality and not wanting to be challenged by his younger nephew (D. Hall 132). What dominance Black men exerted was tied, like that of their masters to their ability to use their job status as a route to practice individualistic patriarchy. However, a major blow to their dominance was that Black men could not protect Black women from (sexual) violence and predation of white men. White men slept with the wives, daughters, mothers and sisters of stolen African men and thus were taunted for their subjugated position. Some slave men overtly remonstrated against being diminished in the lives of their women (D. Hall 50). Lincoln perhaps acts out the frustration in more covert, 'safer' ways for Black men when he allows Sally to run from Thistlewood's sexual abuse (199).

Black Men and Labour

The psychological turmoil inflicted on Black men and boys (as with girls), in Barbados and the CC started early. Slavery deprived Black boys and girls of childhood. Thistlewood's records reveal boys being apprenticed to learn trades as early as seven and a half (D. Hall 272; Patterson 156). Black boys were forced into childhood labour, they did not enjoy play and child appropriate activity. Many of the complaints Thistlewood had about Jimmy could be categorized as the curiosity and mischievousness of childhood discovery (D. Hall 203–4). Thistlewood's account of Jimmy also reveals that Black boys were sexualized at young ages just like girls. Jimmy got his first bout of venereal disease at fifteen or sixteen (D. Hall 203–4). Chub also has his first battle with venereal disease at fifteen, remains lame and dies in nine years (T. Burnard 191; 192). Venereal disease, back breaking work and starvation accounted for a usually short life spans of Black men. Many men also turned to the very byproduct they were producing – rum – to drown their pain and sorrow (D. Hall 146; 201).

According to Richard Dunn, there were a variety of diseases that plagued Black Africans and the English in the CC (Dunn 300–6). Black men died faster than Black women because their physical labour capacity was brutally exploited; they were more likely to go malnourished. Men were largely expected to find their own subsistence; they suffered more fatal accidents in the making of sugar and other types of work on plantation; they were brutally treated for expressing anger, agency or for survival tactics like stealing and they were often flogged, maimed and executed in response to infractions (317). The prospects for Black men were dire under the plantation system, although the seven-year-old who was learning carpentry had a better chance than his peer assigned to a field gang. Learning a trade such as carpentry offered more social mobility than being a field hand. Lincoln is able to command his own time and conditions with Thistlewood because he was a skilled marksman and fisherman (T. Burnard 197). Lincoln also gets to bear arms and given the significant legal restrictions the Black population lived with this was a 'privilege'. The number of white versus Black people in the territories under British rule means other men, including head slaves and drivers may also have had access to weapons (198). The corollary to the personal freedoms granted to certain Black men was the overall divisionary tactics to ensure that Black male solidarity did not effervesce to repudiate white rule. The individual rights gained by some men caused mistrust and discontent among Black men in general. The discontent and mistrust fuelled by disparate privileges given to Black men by social/work/class categories specifically and other enslaved Africans more broadly has survived into the contemporary CC. One of the major ways that white power has been upheld in the CC is through the granting of unequal privileges to Black people in such a way that makes them fight among each other and not together. The privilege that job status brought to

Thistlewood's slaves and that it brings in contemporary Caribbean society is short lived. In the case of Black manhood, small and often manipulative privileges are not enough to change the status of Black manhood as a subjugated category in plantation society. Of Lincoln, Burnard writes that, "Thistlewood intruded constantly in Lincoln's life" (195). The slave master's interference in the lives of Black men has been replaced by police mistreatment and surveillance especially of men in at risk communities; lack of economic opportunities and carceral complexes.

Polygamy or Dysfunction?

Given that he had no real autonomy beyond what was bequeathed to him, could Lincoln be a polygamist? Several male commentators on CC history have made a case for polygamy as an African social and cultural retention (T. Burnard 189–90; Patterson 107; Beckles, *Natural Rebels* 117). Linguists in working through the elements of African language retention in Creole languages argue that the features common across African languages are the ones that survived in the Caribbean (Allsop xxxi; Cassidy xxxviii). Can the same kind of argument be applied to the social practice, what is called polygamy, in early plantation society or even now? For sure, polygamy was practised in premodern societies including African ones (Lerner 170). Notwithstanding the continued sexual freedom of men, Lerner also notes that polygamy "later became rare except for royalty, and monogamous marriage became the ideal and the rule" (Lerner 170). Thus, the practice of polygamy in Africa was not within the reach of every African man and the extent to which it was in the reach of the ones stolen and brought to the Caribbean is highly questionable. I believe what is more important, is that while men may have curtailed their engagement with women as Gerda outlines, what remained constant was male domination over women. I do not see a crucial purpose for reading polygamy into the CC plantation context as a remnant of Africa. What I do believe is that domination over women and the sexual freedom men had in premodern societies was a feature of both African and European societies. Sexual freedom and domination of women as male practice are transplanted and are present in CC plantation societies. Something more happens in Caribbean societies. Along with the sexual freedom of men, there are also incentives for women to be sexually free including maintaining autonomy and financial gain. The behaviour of having multiple sexual relations expands beyond polygamy and I suggest a more accurate term for what occurs in the Caribbean plantation society is multi-partnering. While white men had the means and status to support their lifestyle, Black men were left frustrated – fighting to be relevant to women whom they had no legal status over in the case of white ones or Black ones who they could not help the financial way that would command polygamous loyalty. My discomfort is that labelling the multi-partnering relationships that develop on plantation as polygamy might be a conflation. It also negates the fact that multi-partnering is not gender specific or reserved for men.

Even with a historical we use historical definitions of polygamy, I believe that the multi-partnering of Black men in PPC throws up a more complex situation. Individualistic patriarchy can support multi-partnering but not polygamy because individualistic patriarchs are disconnected from real financial and structural power to maintain households. During slavery white men were the patriarchs. Black men mimicked their patterns and behaviours of having multiple households but without autonomy or a way to sustain them. Trevor Burnard reads Abba as a polygamous possession of Lincoln (188). However he is forced to correct his misinterpretation (222). Abba was a single woman who multi-partnered for its financial gains and perhaps to find sexual satisfaction. After losing the battle to make a polygamy fit a situation which it ill describes, Burnard reads women in the Caribbean (and I agree) as forming their own performances of womanhood unique to the Caribbean space and best not read as African retentions. He explains:

> It was not so much that slave (SIC) women were powerful as that slave (SIC) men were powerless. The peculiar conditions of slavery rendered black men's attempts to control the sexuality of black women problematic. Women often insisted on their ability to play the field, believed they had the right to stop men from philandering, and were willing to break out of traditional gender arrangements. Male slaves (SIC) attempted to place limits on these newfound female freedoms. (204)

Polygamy is a non-gendered term in contemporary usage but most of the writers on CC familial structures seem to only attribute the behaviour to men. The term multi-partnering moves us beyond this cultural, gendered definition to account for the fact that both Black men and Black women in plantation culture multi-partner. Men's motive may be connected to performance of dominant masculinities requiring subjugation of women and women's reasons may have links to the financial inability of men to provide adequately on plantation. Both men and women sought sexual gratification and satisfaction from at least one or more of their partners. Burnard concludes that "the brutality, flux, and trauma of slave life made family life and community life highly dysfunctional" (236). Multi-partnering that destabilizes family and leads to the spread of venereal disease is dysfunctional. Polygamy between consenting adults is not – another simple reason why what happened and happens in the CC is not accurately categorized as polygamy.

One of the significant fallouts plantation society dysfunction was and is its effects on Black parenthood in general and fatherhood in particular. Where Black women may have been given a bit of time with their children after birth, and where measures to encourage natural increase of the African labour force on plantation gave Black women a modicum of hope not to be separated from their children, there was nothing standing between the Black father and separation from children. Black men were proud to be fathers and were emotionally connected to their children. Strap sought and got permission from Thistlewood to bury his dead child (D. Hall 294). However, subjugated manhood and lack of autonomy resulted in Black fathers not being able to care their progeny. This is especially true for men who were labelled 'breeders'. The numbers of children they had made it impossible for them to care their offspring either emotionally or financially (Foster, *Rethinking Rufus* 61). Multi-partnering, legitimated by Massa for the benefit of increased labour force, robbed Black men of closeness with their children and an opportunity to germinate a fatherhood that was nurturing and uplifting. Absentee fatherhood has created a vicious cycle in CC plantation societies where boys especially are emotionally wrecked by the abandonment of their fathers and then men who due to their childhood wounds wreck the next generation they sire.

The Black male body has endured severe physical damage through whippings, mutilation and execution. Along with the physical, there was also real and lasting damage in the emotional and psychological realms. Where Butch heterosexuality is a performance of womanhood that allowed women to ring-fence themselves from the worst emotional and psychological perils of plantation, there wasn't much that men could alter to rescue Black masculinity and make it a safe, inhabitable space. Even within maroon masculinity, the resistance to enslavement comes at the expense of breaking ranks with other Black men to be the gate keeper of white supremacy and dominance. To be a good man in plantation is to become an individualist patriarch. It was to be self-centred, cruel, sexually abusive, manipulative not just at the personal level but also at the systemic level through systems of power and to be emotionally dead. Glimpses of Black men's emotional unavailability and the relationship disruption caused by it are seen in rolling stone Jimmy's life portrait (D. Hall 185). Thomas Foster unmasks the deep emotional trauma that being chosen for a breeding man had on Black men (Foster, *Rethinking Rufus* 55–63). The role disrupted family and community life and left those men devoid of stability and emotional comfort. Burnard reads a similar type of disruption to family life in the case of Abba – Thistlewood's most fertile kidnapped African (222). Emotional unavailability became an afterlife of the deep and pervasive plantation violence.

White Women and Plantation

White women are the epitome of the adage, "hurt people, hurt people". White women were completely displaced in the CC individualist patriarchal system. While there were the other side of the dichotomy that created white masculinity and supremacy in theory, practically they were dispensable. White men were busy living out their every fetish with Black women who were exotic and legally could not resist their white owners. The hardships of white women resulted in a bitter brutality. White men turned a blind eye to the abuse caused by white women's hurt egos because it allowed them even more unfettered access to fulfilling their fetishes. The brutality of white women cohabited with their roles of mother and wife (C. Hall 76). The literature is replete with images of the savagery caused by hurt, white female ego:

> Although James Randolph had sworn Elizabeth to secrecy regarding the paternity of her "white" baby, Mrs. Randolph could see for herself that Louisa had a remarkable resemblance to her own infant, born only two weeks earlier. Mrs. Randolph insisted that Elizabeth and her child be sold. (Stevenson 159)

Another example is the experience of Sophia Pooley, a Black woman who went from the United States to Canada:

> Brant's third wife, my mistress, was a barbarous creature. She could talk English, but she would not. She would tell me in Indian to do things, and then hit me with anything that came to hand, because I did not understand her. I have a scar on my head from a wound she gave me with a hatchet; and this long scar over my eye, is where she cut me with a knife. The skin dropped over my eye… (Drew 194)

When the violence of white, hurt female ego was not directly exacted, it prevailed through the villainization of the 'strong' Black woman and Black womanhood in general. White women were in the vanguard of painting Black women as damaged.

> I regret to say it, that female negroes are far more unmanageable than males. The little girls are far more wicked than the boys and I am convinced that were every proprietor to produce the list of his good negroes, there would be, in every instance an amazing majority in favour of males. Mrs. A Carmichael reproduced in (T. Burnard 209).

And

> We know Betsy well. Has she soul enough to swear by? She is a great stout, jolly, irresponsible, unreliable, pleasant-tempered, bad-behaved woman with ever so many good points. Among others, she is so clever she can do anything. And she never loses her temper but she has no moral sense whatever. Chesnut reproduced in (Glymph 98)

These views about Black women, are the ones that white women used to justify exploitation Black women. White women had no problem, just like white men, in accumulating the gains of Black women's sexual labour. Hilary

Beckles notes that in Barbados some white women were able to maintain themselves running brothels, literally and figuratively on the backs of Black women (*Natural Rebels* 143). Catherine Hall reports a similar situation in Jamaica (C. Hall 79). Thomas Foster reminds us that white women also used their position of dominance to force Black men into unequal sexual relations (Foster, "The Sexual Abuse of Black Men under American Slavery" 125). The double standards and misplaced vexation with their husband's philandering were a major underpinning of the quest to 'Christianize' Black women in the CC. White women hoped to regain their lost place in plantation societies by curbing unfettered sex and cajoling white men to proper family values. Christian principles made it so that could only be achieved by marrying good and graceful white women. The same white men and women who withheld Christianity from enslaved Africans in the CC at the height of chattel slavery, suddenly had much usefulness for it at legal emancipation (C. Hall 18–20; 86–7; 331–2).

The ill will of white women towards Black women continues in the way that white women treat Black women in the workforce and in other interactions. Thavolia Glymph outlines the contempt and white attitudes directed at Black women in the Reconstruction era of the United States of America (Glymph 210). Colleen Vasconcellos points to similar sentiments of white women towards Black women in the Caribbean (46). White women have tried to erase Black women's contributions to global women's organizing movements. Black women's contributions to anti-patriarchal, pro-woman, intellectual theory and content have been claimed as feminist – whether Black women intended their work to be feminist or not. This pervasive and systematic anti-Black racism underpinned Sojourner Truth's now world-famous question. It has created impetus for the work of other Black writers such as bell hooks and Audre Lorde who have explored the theme. As I have noted it is for these reasons that feminism holds no currency for me as an analytic that can help Black Caribbean women to resist individualistic patriarchy. My way is mine but I also leave space – every soul has to find her own positioning in the project of her freedom.

Black Women and Plantation

The unravelling of Black women's experiences with plantation, both as a historical and contemporary phenomenon is one that shows the true value of two-handed reading. In between the academic arguments that paint Black women in plantation societies as either total victim or free agent personifying ultimate sexual agency, is reality – Black women in PPC were and are subjugated and oppressed by individualistic patriarchy and she has found ways to rebel and embrace life and livingness inside and beyond the bedroom. As Douglas reminds us, one of the benefits of Thomas Thistlewood's diaries is that they give us a view of PPC that was not elitist. In that view there is less rigidity in the social relations in daily life on the plantation (D. Hall 25). It is in these middling views that the best glimpses of the emergence of butch heterosexuality in PPC emerge. If hegemonic views of gender performance are used to interpret the lives of middle and underclasses in PPC, harmful errors occur such as Trevor Burnard makes in constantly classifying Phibbah, the Black common law wife of Thomas Thistlewood, as his mistress (T. Burnard 181; 185). The relationship Thistlewood shares with Phibbah contrasts to those recorded in other plantation environments where mistresses were set up in separate housing and alongside legal wives (Stevenson 168; 172). The differences in the competence to offer nuanced interpretations of the Thistlewood diaries between Trevor Burnard's *Mastery, Tyranny and Desire* and Douglas Hall's *In Miserable Slavery* bear out the point that Caribbean intellectuals have long made that insider lived experience is key to accurate representations of the culture of the Caribbean. The misrepresentations are not trivial. They obscure Black womanhood and disconnect us from our ancestors and their resistance/survival mechanisms.

As outlined in the section above, there were few gains for individualistic patriarchs to be married. Many, like Thistlewood never bothered to and cohabited instead with their lovers. The absence of marriage sanctioned by the state or church has long been a matter of contention, defence and debate in the Caribbean. Phibbah is perhaps one of the earliest recorded common law wives in the CC – a status that many Black women in the contemporary Caribbean continue to live. Thistlewood's diaries make it clear that he was not shy about paying for sex even before he left England (D. Hall 4; 7; 9). He also continues paying for casual sex with women, some of whom he kept as mistresses, throughout his life (D. Hall 20; 195). His diary also clearly shows that the relationship he shared with 'Phib'[7] was far more than he shared with his mistresses. Thistlewood courts Phibbah (D. Hall 61). The couple enjoyed a robust sex life that lasted over three decades. They shared co-parentship over their child, John and were business associates. Phibbah assisted Thistlewood in the purchase and organization of Breadnut pen and protects his business interest. On several occasions, Phibbah lends Thistlewood money (D. Hall 94; 117; 143; 218; 219; 227).

Phibbah the Businesswoman

Readers get access to the life of Phibbah through her relationship with Thistlewood but it clearly emerges that she is her own woman much like the characters of Hilary Beckles' *Natural Rebels.* Phibbah used her position in Thistlewood's life to solidify her independence rather than depend on him financially. She learns to tame her emotions and keeps them open. Rather than make a fuss about who Thistlewood was as a man, she too multi-partnered and maintained her individuality in their relationship. Phibbah has her own money and her own sphere of influence, including her children, other Black women and white women. It is these characteristics that I am paying attention to for the possibilities they give us for an alternate womanhood beyond received gender norms. To focus on Phibbah and Thistlewood's sexual relationship only occludes other roles of value to white men that Black women performed in PPC. Just like men had certain trades that allowed them more freedom and prestige so too there were a set of job options that provided Black women to perform a womanhood that had emergent patterns of self-sufficiency.

While I believe that Lucille Mathurin-Mair's article "Reluctant Matriarchs" is a useful and important intervention in understanding Black womanhood in the Caribbean, she and I differ on the impact of job privilege for Black[8] women in PPC. Mathurin-Mair suggests that the only two 'semi-professional' jobs Black women had access to on the plantation were nurse and midwife. She notes that domestic work was another option but the women performing it were little more than "superannuated field workers" (Mathurin-Mair 132). I think there is a need to straighten some overgeneralizations. First, the distinctions between house and field may have been more overstated than the actual, daily experience of our ancestors. Thistlewood's diaries show constant 'demotions' and 'promotions' from fieldwork to housework and vice versa (D. Hall 192; 198–9; 228). Beckles corroborates the pattern (Beckles, *Natural Rebels* 56). Thus, colourism alone may not have been enough to shield a woman from demotion or guarantee work 'inside'. Neither Vine nor Phibbah was mulatto and they both had jobs that afforded them job privilege. Both Mathurin-Mair and Beckles highlight the complex connection between job proximity to whiteness and the desire of Black workers to be themselves more white and assimilated (Mathurin-Mair 132; Beckles, *Natural Rebels* 67–8). Notwithstanding, it would be erroneous to assume that every woman who occupied close work proximity to whiteness automatically accepted white superiority. Second, even if job privilege was rigidly tied to mulatto features during the 1700s, the period Mathurin-Mair and Thistlewood are concerned with, mulattos have 'strike back' children who would have been considered Black but who would have been raised in that socio-economic class. Thus, in the second period of gender relations – after legal emancipation – it is these very jobs that I am arguing women had access to that created a nascent self-sufficiency which became the economic underpinning of reluctant matriarchs. In other words, even though I do not overstate women's access to job privilege at earlier periods in the plantation experience, it becomes more visible at other temporal moments. These jobs and the self-sufficiency they allow enable butch heterosexuality. Women could renegotiate gender roles when they have mite to support themselves and their children beyond individualistic patriarchs. Some of the other semi-professions available to Black women were/are:

Seamstress – Thistlewood records Phibbah's sewing as part of his income (D. Hall 170)

(Executive) Assistant – Thistlewood talks to Phibbah. He trusts her to oversee workmen. Vine was left in charge of Sameul Say's pen when he takes an overseer's job. (D. Hall 80; 136; 144; 226; Beckles, *Natural Rebels* 65–6).

Higgler (small-scale redistributor)/sales associate-Phibbah and other women move stock for Thistlewood. They sold crabs, provisions from his gardens, fish, cuts of neat, cloth and items of clothing (D. Hall 120; 156; 165; Beckles, *Natural Rebels* 72).

Logistics handler – Thistlewood records Phibbah and other women helping him to unpack items he receives from England and sorting them for sale (D. Hall 225).

Entertainer – Thistlewood was entertained by women telling Anasi stories. Storytelling was an important pastime in plantation society (D. Hall 160).

Manager-Phibbah's substantive job was manager of Egypt great house cook room which obviously afforded her privileges including making her own money (D. Hall 31; 60; 94; Beckles, *Natural Rebels* 58). Thistlewood also seems to privilege Abba as his Chief domestic and equivalent to what Phibbah's job at Egypt (D. Hall 186).

Cook – This individual co-ordinated the supplies needed to ensure meals were prepared including when hosting was done. Cooking was a task that showed the vulnerability of 'white society' to the unfree. Food could deliver nourishment or annihilation. It is perhaps partly for preservation that the jobs of 'cook' and 'housekeeper' were entangled in wider sexual relationships (Beckles, *Natural Rebels* 59; 64–5). Cooking delicacies for sale was also a way to earn income (D. Hall 231; Beckles, *Natural Rebels* 73–4).

Small loans financier – There are several examples in Thistlewood's diaries of Phibbah supporting his efforts financially (D. Hall 142; 218; 219; 227; 291).

Business coach – Thistlewood learns the art of higgling from Black women (D. Hall 121).

These roles are not thought of as leadership or privileged because they were and still are undervalued. They are firmly caught in the quagmire of women's unpaid care work and emotional labour. Along with jobs close to whiteness that allowed women privilege, a smaller group of women may have become respected enough to perform in leadership roles in the field gangs. When Thistlewood is frustrated at the performance of his male drivers, Phoeba becomes driver for a stint (D. Hall 291). The role of driver is often casted as a male position of privilege but Hilary Beckles also documents women drivers in Barbados (*Natural Rebels* 55). Moreover, woman were almost always responsible for the "hogmeat" gang[9] – a plantation work group for the youngest children. Although her role is essentially the same as the drivers of the first, second and third gang, her role was feminized due to the care work associated with children. Additionally, while Caribbean intellectual, Douglas Hall, documents Phoeba in the position of driver, foreign scholar Trevor Burnard does not mention this display of woman leadership beyond housework at all.[10] Alas, as astute an archivist as Beckles is, head driver women remain faceless and nameless. As in the case of their male counterparts, it is hard to believe that female drivers would not have shown up in the archive even if it was just by name and work task – in fact they would have had to for Beckles to be able to write their existence. Perhaps a return to the archive with fresh eyes for women's roles in the field enterprise of plantation could yield much.

In *Natural Rebels,* Hilary Beckles focused on the prevalence of sex work in Barbados. Sex work is clearly an important occupation in the plantation world – both for white women and Black women in and beyond the Caribbean. Most of the white women sent to the Caribbean were sex workers 'cleaned' up off the streets of the metropole (Beckles, *Natural Rebels* 57; Wilson 141–2). There is no need for me to argue that sex work was not as important as it was on the plantation. What I do want to make space for is that even when women accepted sex work as a viable option, they still resisted and sought advantage in their condition as Mr. Drummond discovers:

> Going through the Savanna, [Mr. Drummond] met with a Negro wench who said she belonged to Mr. Stone and agreed to go among the bushes together, where, when they had got, she desired payment first, upon which he pulled out his purse of knitted green silk, through which she easily saw his money (being about 20 pistoles in it), and holding it rather carelessly, she snatched it out of his hand starting immediately; and he has never since heard of it, nor does he think he should know the girl again (D. Hall 224–5).

The survival tactics and guile of Black women were labelled as wicked or hostile (and became stereotypes of Black womanhood across the board). Some would have developed a womanhood laced with submission, supplication and acquiescence to be successful at sex work, others developed a womanhood that was more masculine in orientation and steeped in self-sufficiency, refusal and autonomy. Similar to the way that individualistic patriarchy made white men fiercely defensive of their unfettered and unchallenged sovereignty, Black women too, as the most subjugated racial/gendered position of plantation came to value refusal and autonomy as important elements of their freedom. I am not arguing for a performance of womanhood as better than another, just that both exist/ed. Given the extent of sexual brutality that Black women faced on the plantation, it is legitimate that a kind of femininity that elevated self-reliance and sex as choice and not force would emerge. Examples are seen in Rose William's testimony of being a 'breeder'.

After Emancipation, Rose decided that she was not going to have relations with men (Doddington 153). It is a sentiment and a practice that pervaded Black women's performances of womanhood in the CC and the wider African Diaspora. Kamau Brathwaite in explaining the success of the system of racial and gender subjugation that gave rise to PPC, plantation and what he calls creole society explains, "Creole society was stable because the underprivileged within it conformed to the system, its divisions and its restrictions. 'The whole slave system began as a coercive one, but developed into a system of consent'" (Brathwaite 193). Black women, especially after legal Emancipation in the CC have been withholding consent and refusing to remain subjugated to men – Black or white. This has led to a deep resentment between Caribbean men and women, the former feeling they have been robbed by the latter of their opportunity to be individualistic patriarchs. These tensions are explored in Chapters 2 and 3. Womanhood in PPC is not for the faint hearted. Daintiness and proper (white) performances of soft and demure womanhood could not have been the approach of Black women. There was too much abuse, grief and suffering in PPC to make genteel womanhood viable.

Black Women who did not have the ability to be militant and roll with plantation did not thrive. Burnard shows, through his sketch of Sally that 'gentler women' or those who became overwhelmed with plantation life suffered (218–21). There were worse things to be than Butch on a plantation. There were huge hurdles to overall well-being and safety. Violence as a feature of life was as equal to the presence of sugar cane and rum. Many women suffered chronic vaginal and pelvic illnesses due to repeated venereal reinfections and menstrual troubles due in part to undernourishment (D. Hall 217; Patterson 109–10). Carrying a child to term often meant trying to mother the product of rape or forced sex. Death at childbirth was an increased possibility. The extent of child loss from miscarriage or death soon after birth was astronomical. Due to a lack of bodily autonomy, some women did not fully mourn the child lost before they were pregnant again and facing compounded loss due to another death or miscarriage. Thistlewood had sex with Abba as well as her blind daughter, Mary (D. Hall 298). Black women were completely powerless to keep their children safe and sex with young children was a fetish well enjoyed on plantation. Black mothers lived in fear of losing children to death or sale.

The inability to protect children must have resulted in a feeling of complete hopelessness. As Thistlewood's diary revealed not even the sacred time of pregnancy curtailed his sexual predation. He rapes captive Africans when they are heavily pregnant – up to two days before they give birth in instances (D. Hall 186; 195; 283). It follows from the level of sexual abuse present in Barbados and the CC that motherhood was complex. Burnard outlines the suffering of mothers[11] to provide for their children through the experience of Abba (221–7). The complexity of Black motherhood was pathologized (D. Hall 213; Patterson 106–7). As refusal and coping strategy, Black women took measures to ensure they either did not fall pregnant or could abort pregnancies expediently (D. Hall 145; Patterson 108; Sheller 57). The extent of the loss and how it affected most of the women under Thistlewood's dominion is a recurrent theme throughout his diary. Motherhood also meant deeper impoverishment in the context where daily subsistence needs were not met for most kidnapped Africans.

Conclusion

This chapter is a reading of available literature about gender and sexual relations not just across the Caribbean but also the United States inter alia, Thomas Foster's, *Rethinking Rufus: Sexual Violations of Enslaved Men;* Emily Owens' *Consent in the Presence of Force: Sexual Violence and Black Women's Survival in Antebellum New Orleans*; Daina Berry and Leslie Harris's *Sexuality & Slavery: Reclaiming Intimate Histories in the Americas* and Joy Degruy's *Post Traumatic Slave Syndrome: America's Legacy of Enduring Injury & Healing.* While this kind of pan-examination of the system of slavery would be problematic in some kinds of study about plantation, it works in the context of understanding more about gender relations and sexuality. It gets us beyond significant gaps in historical record (Dunn xxv). The pan-examination works because sex, sex as power, satisfaction of fetish, curiosity and performance of patriarchal manhood were ever present and pervasive wherever masters and subjugated Africans were in contact. As Brenda Stevenson explains:

> Sexual contact between slave master and their bonded female "property" was a common experience in the Atlantic world. These relations ran the gamut from rape and sodomy to romance, from chance encounters to obsession, concubinage and even "marriage." They could be hetero- or homosexual in nature. They included, but were not limited to, pedophilia, incest, sadomaschoism, and voyeurism. One need only pursue the travel literature, diaries, church records, letters, and even colonial newspapers produced throughout French, British, Dutch, Portuguese, and Spanish American colonies to find ample evidence. Whether one reads the diary of William Byrd of early eighteenth-century Virginia or Thomas Thistlewood of eighteenth-century Jamaica, Olaudah Equiano's writings descriptive of live in Montserrat, or John Steadman's account of his life in late eighteenth-century Suriname provide details and descriptions. In the travel accounts of other curious European onlookers in the Americas; ecclesiastical records of the Catholic Church in Florida, Brazil, Cuba, New Orleans, and New Spain; printed abolitionist attacks on the immoral consequences of slavery, and, for that matter, Thomas Jefferson's *Notes* on the same topic; as well as hundreds of recollections and autobiographical accounts of enslaved people in the Atlantic World, one is confounded by the prevalence of sexual contact between European or European American men [and European Caribbean men] and African or African American women [and African Caribbean women] bound by the institution of slavery. It was a common occurrence by any measure, widespread and obvious. (Stevenson 160–1)

Where pan-examination strategies are used to fill gaps about gender and sexuality on plantation, care has to be paid to declaring nuances. Shared use of the documented historical experiences of plantation does not justify conflation of gender and sexual performances or relations of Diasporic Black people. For instance, while there was at least some reputational risk to men being in relations with Black or mulatto women outside of their marriages in the United States context, no such impediment resulted in the Caribbean context (Stevenson 170). Trevor Burnard offers expansion that clarifies Stevenson's point. Where American society was controlled under a hierarchy of gentlemen, in Jamaica white was mite and that was that:

> [The] shift form patriarchalism to paternalism never occurred in Jamaica [and the CC]. It remained a patriarchal rather than a paternal society throughout the eighteenth century. Moreover, it remained a society with a particular variant of patriarchalism, derived from its peculiar demography and unusual social relationships. Patriarchalism was very raw in Jamaica [and the CC]. White men there were less concerned than white men elsewhere in the British world with making sure that their authority was tempered by an understanding that patriarchs had to recognize mutual obligations between household heads and dependents. Jamaican men [and men in the CC] refused to accept any constraints on their freedom to act as they chose, least of all constraints placed on them by dependents. Patriarchy was not shaped by concepts of stewardship but was "the manifestation and institutionalisation" of raw male dominance, with scant regard to the duties men owed to others. What made Jamaican [and CCean] patriarchalism unique was that white male dominance could be exerted only over **women, children and slaves**. It could not be exercised over independent white men. Thus, patriarchy was Janus-faced. It looked backward to ancient notions of patriarchy that assumed that dominant men could do whatever they pleased to inferiors. (84)

Individualistic patriarchy is connected to proto-patriarchy but two-handed reading applied reveals that it is also a rupture in patriarchy. To interpret what happened in the Caribbean based on traditional patriarchal norms is to miss a burgeoning masculine femininity. Moreover, it is to miss the fact that patriarchy becomes raced in ways that it was not before PPC. Individualistic patriarchy is a grafting of ancient patriarchal gains with white supremacy and if proto-patriarchy was bad for women before, individualistic patriarchy arising from the CC plantation experience was the solidification of a double subjugation of – racial and gendered – that has changed the complete life trajectory of Black men, boys, women and girls. White patriarchs in the CC world were some of the most unchecked anywhere in human history. They were brutal and brutish. They used everything – Bible, threat, death and whip in service of their egos. The systems that they set up – political and juridical – were not established to serve the needs of people. They were set up to legitimate corruption and enrich white men as much as possible.

Has the emotional fallout from the brutality of the mechanisms of slavery in the CC, the impacts on gender performance and plantation sexual contact been researched enough? Those impacts are embedded in our history, but equally in contemporary possibilities. Why does the only type of femininity conjured is a delicate, supplicant femininity when the experience of plantation clearly shows it demanded something different? Would supplicant femininity not have been devoured by brutes? The answer lies partly in the difficulty with finding records to support expansive performances of womanhood. Writers of CC history have focused more on sex than gender performance and even with sex – it is done clandestinely and often leaves little trace (Downs 189; 90). Another answer is that many of the researchers studying Caribbean plantation have been men. Particularly in the work of Hilary Beckles there is an interpretation of archives which upholds the problematic masculinities. It is unlikely that women's resistance or other performances of gender that did not uphold the narrative would be of interest. Downs encourages us, following Elizabeth Alexander, to consider whether the silences in the archive around Black women's sexuality could have been an act of agency on their part (192–3). Even if this is seen as somewhat of a stretch, I do agree with him that the question "would these women approve of the ways in which historians, all of whom possess well-meaning intentions, dig up details about their intimate lives?" is one of respect and is important to ponder (192–3). Hilary Beckles reads the 'power' that slave women had in their sexuality but he does not move his reading beyond rabid sex to the legitimacy that a woman has when a man develops feelings for her. In this way Beckles, perhaps quite unintentionally, contributes to the dehumanization and objectification of Caribbean women. As Douglas Hall reveals to us, Phibbah perhaps had some power to reduce Thistlewood's use of fetishized punishments not just because she had sex with Thistlewood, but because he developed feelings for her. It is my hope that a new crop of researchers interested in gender and womanhood in the Caribbean return to the archives for what may have been left out or misinterpreted.

Despite the challenges with finding records as Downs aptly put it, representing our ancestors is a work of rehumanizing them. Writing and thinking about them as more than 'economic units' offers better understanding of them and ourselves (192–3). Rehumanizing our ancestors provides valuable information that explain CC approaches to life – womanhood, manhood, family and gender relations – past and present. The 'power' that Black Caribbean women had during slavery does not have to be overstated to understand and accept that those kernels of resistance and resilience birthed in slavery ratooned their way into current performances of gender and womanhood in the contemporary Caribbean. Reaching back into the archives stands to not only provide understanding of Caribbean womanhood. Perhaps Caribbean men can work through some of the generational trauma that keeps them emotionally walled off and invested in a masculinity that emerged from debauchery and extreme oppression. Maybe the fraught racial relations in Barbados can be adjusted by talking through the unresolved tensions between Black and white women and white men and all other gender categories in the society. That conversation should proceed in a way that allows non-traditional performances of womanhood – including butch heterosexuality to feature in questions and answers.

Notes

1 See newspaper articles such as https://torontocaribbean.com/appalling-situation-at-government-industrial-school-barbados/, https://barbadostoday.bb/2021/03/16/ministry-launches-probe-at-reform-school/, https://barbadostoday.bb/2021/03/25/btcolumn-the-government-industrial-school-issue-2/. The issue was picked up in local, regional and international media spaces.
2 *In Miserable Slavery: Thomas Thistlewood in Jamaica 1750–86* (Hall).
3 *Mastery, Tyranny, and Desire: Thomas Thistlewood and his Slaves in the Anglo-Jamaican World* (T. Burnard).
4 Lucille Mathurin Mair reminds us that many women who served as mistresses were mulatto women and not Black women (132). I think it is a valuable point not to conflate Black and mulatto women in the context of the CC plantation society, colourism and impacts on gender performances/sexuality.
5 See Chapter 6 of Douglas Hall's *In Miserable Slavery: Thomas Thistlewood in Jamaica 1750–86* for commentary on the extent of Phibbas' integration in Thistlewood's Business (115–47).
6 Where Carol Pateman suggests that paternal patriarchy becomes fraternal patriarchy in modernity, I argue that individualistic patriarchy was the legacy of contact in the Atlantic World (3).
7 This is Thistlewood's pet name for Phibbah in his Diary entries.
8 Mair is separating Black women from mulatto women. I do believe that the colourism point is an important one to make. I think it may have been slightly overstated in understanding the jobs available to women.
9 See Patterson (59).
10 See my comment above on the differences between Caribbean intellectuals and other writers.
11 More on Black Caribbean motherhood in Chapters 3 and 4.

2 Breaking Silence

State/Family Dysfunction and Plantation

Chapter 1 explored the effects of plantation on individual actors in Commonwealth Caribbean (CC) plantation society. Setting out individualistic patriarchy and its effects on various categories of gendered identities is germinal to understanding how plantation remains embedded and operational in the contemporary Caribbean. Plantation logics still govern major social aspects including gender relations and how the arising impacts – gender tensions and violence – are perceived and addressed. The emergent womanhood and manhood shown by Doll, Abba and other kidnapped Africans in Thomas Thistlewood's diaries and other analyses of the Jamaican, Barbadian and Guyanese societies ratoon, refine and strengthen in subsequent CC historical periods. Butch Heterosexuality becomes a viable interspace to preserve life, limb and mind in the violence of plantation society.

Writers trying to explain and understand the Black experience have positioned themselves on two sides of a dichotomy – either unctuous approval of the way Caribbean people survived slavery and rebuilt their families or laments over the dysfunction with blame raining the Caribbean family – everything including the size of families; to the poverty usually present, to the people 'missing' from the family. While I am troubling the ideological technologies that keep butchness and heterosexuality at oppositional distance I likewise hope to destabilize the idea that the Caribbean family unit is either all good and manifest of resilience and a Caribbean identity or all dysfunctional due to the 'wickedness' of Black people. The Caribbean is a beautiful, resourceful complex that emerged resulting from the worst depravity in human history. Many of the logics that underpinned the making of Blackness in the Transatlantic slave trade re-emerge in neoliberal interference that exploits natural and human resources for the enrichment of (absentee) capitalists. The Caribbean is interpreted as part of a third world – problematic, broken but also carrying potential if it can be rescued from the problems that are seen as the problems of Blackness but are actually the remnants of the violence and brutality used to form the post-1492 modernity.

Rightfully so, Caribbean intellectuals have offered theories and perspectives designed to bolster Caribbean culture and pride. The unhelpful byproduct

DOI: 10.4324/9781003518709-3

of that perhaps is not allowing a call out of dysfunction in plantation societies or developing strategies to address it. To say that Caribbean people and families in the Caribbean are not dysfunctional is not the same as saying that there are no relics of dysfunction left in Caribbean gender and other types of social relations. Deborah Thomas makes this distinction and articulates it well in *Exceptional Violence*. While Thomas renounces the thinking that contemporary violence shows any loss of culture or deficiency in younger generations of Jamaicans, she also recognizes violence in Jamaica as a continuity of the spectacular violence of plantation (104–10). In other words, while it is fallacious to portray dysfunction as a racial characteristic, it is also true that the experience of colonialization has resulted in deeply rooted dysfunction in many aspects of Caribbean culture and ways of being. CC society is the remnant of destruction caused by the British colonial experiment. This chapter considers the relic of colonial dysfunction that still affects the family. Family is the main focus and tracing it through changes in the emancipation, independence, immediate post-independence and contemporary trends in Barbados and the CC.

The first section, "Individualistic Patriarchy and State Formation", examines how individualistic patriarchy, the dominant (white) masculinity on plantation was enshrined as the dominant Black masculinity during legal emancipation, nationalist formation and independence. My major argument is that state mechanisms supported individualistic patriarchy and were preserved in Caribbean nationalist ideologies. In the section, "Strong Women and Caribbean Society", gender norms and how the frictions that play out between men and women are examined using information that arises in family court cases. The frictions cause/d deep mistrust between men and women which often characterizes their approaches to family life and can be seen through family court proceedings. The next section, "State Mechanics, Women and Men", takes a closer look at the family court and how it functions. This section contemplates the intersection of building nation, citizenship and colonial relics in relation to the Caribbean family. The final section seeks to bridge the gap between the conceptual and contemporary events in Barbados with the case study of Maude. Her life shows the pervading levels of abuse women experience in Barbados, the complicity of the state and issues that need to be addressed within Barbadian society. A stronger platform for family life and living in Barbados and the CC cannot be attained at the individual, private family level alone. The family problems in the CC are not foreign imports; they are the relics of the formation of CC societies, steeped in dehumanization and violence.

Individualistic Patriarchy and State Formation

One of the major theories of Black manhood to emerge in the Caribbean was Errol Miller's Black marginalization theory. Miller contends that there have been concerted efforts to displace and disenfranchise Caribbean men (8).

Interestingly, men in Jamaica did not recognize their marginalization until women were admitted to the Teaching Service and then became preferred as elementary school teachers. This is because one of the ways that colonial logics coopted Black men and divided unity between them and Black women was to encourage Black men to invest in individualistic patriarchal values and to believe that legal emancipation was their time to experience this kind of headship. Some may ask why I return to the male marginalization theory as an analytical point in this current work since critics have comprehensively debunked it over the years. I return to Black male marginalization theory for two reasons. First the theory is alive and well in the hearts of Barbadian men – even younger men who may not know of Errol Miller reproduce aspects of his theory in explaining their current struggle. I believe that the popularity of the theory gives rise to the second reason I want to return to the theory. While there are useful and important lessons in Miller's marginalization theory, his desire to blame Black women for men's reality overshadows those. Individualist patriarchy and how it is maintained as a tool in the preservation of the politourgeoisie is an underdeveloped but important theme.

The notion that Black men should become patriarchal heads of households was one of the colonial strategies used to keep the Black family broken and disjointed in the period of emancipation. Black men did not recognize the ploy for what it was because it gave them full access to a patriarchy that was germinated in them as a part of their colonial experience. bell hooks explains that:

> When we read annals of history, the autobiographical writings of free and enslaved black men, it is revealed that initially black males did not see themselves as sharing the same standpoint as white men about the nature of masculinity. Transplanted African men, even those coming from communities where sex roles shaped the division of labor, where the status of men was different and most times higher than that of women, had to be taught to equate their higher status as men with the right to dominate women, **they had to be taught patriarchal masculinity. They had to be taught that it was acceptable to use violence to establish patriarchal power.** The gender politics of slavery and white-supremacist domination of free black men was the school where black men from different African tribes, with different languages and value systems, learned in the "new world," patriarchal masculinity. (*We Real Cool* 2; 3)

The retort to hooks has been that Black men were never patriarchs because they have never had the financial or economic power to be. Angela Saini reminds us that patriarchy has never been 'one flat system' and that understanding male domination recognizes "variations depending on local circumstances" (6). Moreover, Chapter 1 established that individualistic patriarchy does not require a man to have money. Many white men in early Caribbean plantation society had a façade of richness based on nothing real. Like many logics of plantation left in the soil, juridical and political structures of the CC, individualist patriarchal masculinity did not terminate with legal emancipation; it continued. Where traditional patriarchy was cemented in the ownership of land and the ability to provide for his household, individualistic patriarchy was based on credit, whiteness and its veneer. Where traditional patriarchy is land based, individualistic patriarchy is commodified and attaches to any resource – land, a job, social position – that gives the impression of wealth. The underpinnings of individualistic patriarchy are: exercise and satisfaction of unfettered, individual ego; the right to profit from and control the labour of women and girls (expanded from the labour of female family members to any and all women); the use of the state mechanism to uphold rule by force, trickery and brutality.

At legal emancipation, and in subsequent periods, patriarchal headship of households was touted as a solution to 'dysfunction' in Black family life. While dominance in the household was encouraged, Black men were discouraged from challenging the status quo. In other words, Black men were encouraged to expect and demand dominance over their women and children but were also expected to accept their continued role of inferior masculinity. Black men did not have access to jobs or economic possibilities to empower themselves and their families. I am suggesting that the distinction between traditional patriarchy and individualistic patriarchy is subtle, but it is important because it answers the question Black Diasporic men have asked for years – Can Black men be patriarchs since Black men too are subjugated?[1] The question is not whether there was patriarchy in Africa that transplanted to the African Diaspora – although the answer is yes. The question is why Black men continue to be invested in individualistic patriarchy – a creation of white supremacy in early Caribbean plantation society – that has been used to do so much harm to them and Black women.

Where bell hooks reports that early framers of Black liberation struggles in the United States were at least willing to comment on and even support women's liberation struggle (as early as 1847), Caribbean men expected Caribbean women to support their liberation by remaining available for male blows and mistreatment (hooks, *We Real Cool* 6). Miller reads Black women in the Caribbean as 'selling out' Black men in his marginalization theory. The truth is, for their taste of dominion over Black women and children, Black men accepted individualistic patriarchy, a role that was ill-suited to the development of the Black woman and the Black family. Black men needed dominion over something based on the model of masculinity available in plantocratic patriarchal culture (PPC). Women and children were the only option for Black Caribbean men. They wanted their turn, and women were the only locus of control Black men had.

The language in Miller's review of teacher education clearly shows that the framers only envisioned their audience as men. Indeed Miller did not find this problematic, and his marginalization thesis is based on his disdain that women dared to want access to teacher training. Black Caribbean men explicate subjugation and marginalization well when it is their own, but they are less adept at recognizing their views and treatment of women as the same colonial carnage that women resisted because it makes life unlivable. Renaldo Walcott notes that the carnage – fused to the logics of emancipation and resulted in a thwarting of freedom (4). To normalize individualistic patriarchy and diminish Black women's resistance to it, Errol Miller, who extolls the harms of 'asociological and ahistorical' accounts of Caribbean history, himself creates an ahistorical and asociological narrative where Black women liked and accepted the subjugation of slavery (74). I am not suggesting that Errol Miller's observation that Black women and men are pitted against each other for the gain of a small elite class, and their prosperity in the Caribbean is not a critical observation – it indeed is. It is an important analysis in fixing a different future for gender and all social relations in the Caribbean. Miller accepts that unity is the only remedy to counteract the undermining of the relationship between the Caribbean Black men and women (76). However, that unification has to be on terms where Caribbean women are seen as full embodied humans and not people who must be willing to capitulate so Caribbean men can thrive.

Black Caribbean men harm themselves when they invest in individualistic patriarchy. I agree with bell hooks that they deprive themselves of wholesome and meaningful relationships (*We Real Cool* xv). That harm is not just at the micro level of the self and the home but also at the level of politics and the society. Orlando Patterson, Kamau Brathwaite and others argue, the CC plantation societies established by individualistic patriarchs barely functioned (Brathwaite 52–7; Patterson 38–9). PPC and individualistic patriarchy and their impact on politics and state functions in Barbados and the CC is an underarticulated topic. The failure of political systems and governance in the CC is a direct result of the characteristics and contradictions of individualistic patriarchy as they exist/ed. Caribbean societies have inherited a governmental system that serves the few and is plagued by corruption. There has also always been a class element that legitimated bourgeoisie ideals of life, and living associated with individualistic patriarchy although it became the masculinity that working-class men aspired to over time. The issue for Black men after emancipation was that while they were told they had freedom in some kind of legal way, freedom did not come with a set of social adjustments that resulted in autonomy. They still had to rent the land of their former enslavers. Restrictions were placed on status markers such as membership to certain (cricket) clubs and property requirements that restrained Black involvement in the political process (Beckles, *A History of Barbados* 199–200; 204; 214; Jemmott 60). Property ownership restrictions resulted in the white planter class maintaining its dominance across the CC. Where Jenny Jemmott locates the post-emancipation interest of Black men in their families in care and pride, I locate it in control and pride (116–17).

Widespread continued exclusion of Black people in the CC post emancipation society resulted in riots in the 1930s. The major struggle that characterized the riots was access to better working conditions, pay, land to farm and build houses and education (Knight, "The Caribbean in the 1930s" 69–71). Simultaneously, Black men were fighting for greater control of their destiny as free men in the Caribbean, the issue of the Black family, and how to manage it was a central research question in North America. Policy makers such as Gunnar Myrdal and Franklin Frazier made a case for more centrality of Black men as the solution to Black social ills and their idea moved into the Caribbean and found ready support (Thomas, *Exceptional Violence* 61–2). Black men were made responsible for the family and the success of it. Instead of seeing this as the setup that it was, because they were not ready either financially or emotionally to take charge of Black families, Black men interpreted this as legitimation of their newfound patriarchal dominance. As Black men favoured themselves as heads of households in the Caribbean, they also fought for independence to be able to fully participate in the financial and political landscape of the region. Nationalism in the CC became a synonym for individualistic patriarchy and PPC.

Individualistic Patriarchy and Caribbean Nationalism

The theories underpinning nationalism and independence in the CC were the same Western ones (including Enlightenment thought) that had produced gendered and racial hierarchies (Allahar 15; Pateman xiv). Put another way, although the labour riots of the 1930 started as a mass movement in ideological contention with plantation, colonialism, capitalism and liberalism, the movement made a pact with the middle and upper classes of the region, perhaps as a strategy to move from protest movement to institutionalized norm. That pact backfired and the space created by worker riots was coopted and returned to the plantation status quo via West Indian 'Anglophiles' such as Errol Barrow of Barbados (Watson 45; 47). The logics of PPC and individualistic patriarchy passed into the independence movement, because as Deborah Thomas' succinctly explains, slavery, colonialism and plantation "generate the terrains of what is possible, examples for roads that might be taken, and norms through which people develop expectation about hierarchy, leadership, and patronage" is insightful because it reveals how past and future enmesh at the point of change (*Exceptional Violence* 48). I am not arguing that every single behavioural pattern of individualistic patriarchy as it was practised by white men passed through to Black individualistic patriarchy although many did. What is more important in understanding the formation of the nationalist Caribbean state is that somebody still had to be dominant (men) and somebody still had to receive the exertion of dominance (women and children). British culture, through mechanisms like education and the church, was still seen as superior, and politics and governance were still characterized by exploitation and spectacular violence as Thomas calls it (*Exceptional Violence* 108–9). Plantation and PPC logics can be seen in the national stories about the formation of independent societies. CC history of nationalist development contributors reads like, "Alexander Bustamante and Norman Manley of Jamaica; Uriah Butler and Albert Gomes of Trinidad; Robert Bradshaw of St. Kitts; Ebenezer Joshua in St. Vincent; Clement Payne and Grantley Adams of Barbados and Vere Bird Sr, from Antigua" (Allahar 26). This despite the fact that women made significant contributions to organizing during this period (Gottlieb 6; Reddock, "Introduction" 5).

As Veronica Gregg explains, "women's experiences …have come to be seen as necessary but peripheral to a putatively larger and more nationalist/Caribbeanist story. Women's lives and contributions have not found their way into the mainstream of the intellectual order" (xv). Colonialism, the experience of Transatlantic slavery and then Black men's investment in individualist patriarchy created a gender divide between Black women and men in the Caribbean. Returning to Errol Miller's male marginalization theory, he suggests that organizing among male teachers was perceived as a threat, and women were brought into teaching to dilute the effort (54–5). Despite what the motives of the colonial authorities may have been, the better question is, why did Caribbean men feel that adding women to the teaching service would dilute their political movement, when Caribbean women have always functioned outside and beyond the public/private gender divide? Veronica Gregg has found an answer to the question in her analysis of George Lamming's *In the Castle of My Skin.* She offers, "the black male Caribbean self-present voice/identity achieves its apparent autonomy mainly through the powerful absent presence of black Caribbean women" (2).

Caribbean men were not concerned that female teachers earned less (Miller 56). In a comparative analysis of the male marginalization thesis in Barbados, historian Aviston Downes noted that while all women headteachers were qualified, some of the men were still operating without qualification (306). Downes then notes that the male marginalization thesis was based on '*perception*' (306) (emphasized in the original). The gap between men's perceptions and the realities of the society requires a two-handed reading approach to be able to properly analyse and understand the nuances of gender norms in the CC. While men built the nationalist society of the CC, with the expectation that Black women should be subjugated for Black men's success, they also convinced themselves that Black women were responsible for their every trouble. The stronger the woman was, the more responsible she was for the demise of the Black man.

Strong Women and Caribbean Society

In the last section I showed how individualistic patriarchy moved from a historical practice into a contemporary practice by showing how men held onto it and brought it onto post Emancipation political and governmental structures and related professions such as teaching. In this section I examine characteristics of female masculinity that moved into post Emancipation and modern societies. Rejecting the hegemonic tendency to create monolithic and dominant identities is an important element in creating new approaches. This section on Caribbean womanhood really considers Black Caribbean women, and other performances of womanhood contextualized by race are beyond the scope of this book.[2] By the time Caribbean women reached Emancipation in Barbados and the Caribbean, they had been working outside the home and figuring out ways to keep themselves and their children alive since the 1600s. Some women opted to live in male-headed households, but as Audre Lorde observes even the ones that did were not in supplicant roles (16). The tendency has been to see Black women's strength as negative because strength and agency are marked as masculine traits. This tendency as I mentioned above has been partly because Black men needed control over women and children to be patriarchs. This theme emerges in the music of the CC. The only plantation Black Caribbean men had access to – still have access to – is the Black woman and children. Access to financial and emotional prowess are difficult to secure in Barbados given how the politourgeoisie closes the system for their narrow gain. Indeed, financial freedom and emotional regulation seem to be elusive for Black men in the Caribbean and thus seem to be accepted as out of reach and lesser desired. Once individualistic patriarchy remains a viable and desirable practice in the CC, women will resist it due to the unsafety it brings.

Available literature reveals more about Caribbean women as mothers than their personhood and agency and how they fought for it. Important studies such as Raymond Smith's *The Negro Family in British Guiana*, Edith Clarke's *My Mother Who Fathered Me,* W. Penn Handwerker's *Women's Power and Social Revolution: Fertility Transition in the West Indies* and Eugene Brody's *Sex Contraception and Motherhood in Jamaica* all focus predominantly on Caribbean women in the role of mother. Far more research is needed on Caribbean women as individual embodied people and not just as mothers. Notwithstanding, there is important information in these studies about women's views and approaches to womanhood. The literature on CC queer women's experiences also offers invaluable information about the ideas underpinning womanhood and agency. The essay "Man Royals and Sodomites" sheds light on the gender struggles faced by women who resist the hierarchical structure of individualistic patriarchy. Unfortunately (and through no fault of the authors), the defiance of queer women is seen to be rooted in their sexual difference rather than an overarching defiance of and claim to agency of women to resist subjugation. However, as I understand the issue that Makeda Silvera raises in her article, it goes far beyond sexual relations.

Silvera explains that while the terms 'man royal' and 'sodomite' were grounded in religious disapproval of queer sexual lifestyle, the term expanded to cover any woman who dared to exist outside of the male gaze and subjugated performances of womanhood (524). I contend that Ms. Bibi is being treated with suspicion not because of her yearly visit from her female friend, but because she likes to read and be alone, behaviours that are not marked as particularly welcoming/womanly (Silvera 525). Ms. Jones has a husband, but she transgresses in a masculine domain with her aesthetic (men's clothing, bare feet) (526–7). Silvera's grandmother's account of Ms. Jones also shows that being lesbian or having a lesbian relationship did not shield women from transactional views of money and survival (526–7). My point here is that gender relations in the Caribbean have always been conflated with sexual relations, and I think this has obscured the ways that Caribbean women have fought for their right to "belong to themselves and each other" (Johnson 10). The women in Silvera's work, whether they had husbands or whether they slept with other women, dared to live inside of aesthetics and behaviours usually walled off as masculine. Women who exercise agency, especially in masculine spaces in the Caribbean, are seen as problematic because they trouble the gender binary. I argue that women who embrace masculinity, strength and agency in their performance of womanhood and heterosexuality are even a bigger threat to the binary and heteronormativity because they expose the myth of masculinity only belonging to men. This is another theme that emerges in the music of the Caribbean.

What is perceived as abhorrent to CC patriarchs is not a same sex orientation. What is unacceptable is a dyke – a name sometimes given to a butch woman in full possession of her own masculine tendencies. Likewise, a heterosexual woman can find herself shunned by Caribbean men generally because of the audacity to possess her own strength, agency or thoughts – all characteristics still marked masculine in the CC. Jack Halberstam reveals the complexity of masculine femininity in queer genealogies (152). Indeed if lesbian butches are forced to forego their masculinity for alignment inside 'female embodiment', what of heterosexual women who can pass given their sexual orientation? They are completely invisible – conflated into lesbians as in Silvera's article. They disappear when Halberstam offers "lesbian, since the rise of lesbian feminism, refers to sexual preference and refers to some version of the "woman-loving woman". Butch, on the other hand, bears a complex relation to femaleness and, in terms of sexual orientation, could refer to a "woman-loving butch" or a butch loving butch"" (Halberstam 153). I want to stretch Halberstam's definition of butchness further and offer Butch heterosexuality as a definitive separation of gender and sexual orientation, thus:

> Butch, on the other hand, bears a complex relation to femaleness and, in terms of sexual orientation, could refer to a woman-loving butch or a butch loving butch **or a butch heterosexual -a Butch loving men**. (Halberstam 153).

Butch heterosexuality, I argue, is to do with how a person performs their gender in relation to societal constellations. Caribbean women did not eschew markers of masculinity because they were valuable to life in PPC and plantation. Men's clothes made it easier to work in agricultural spaces and to protect skin from insect bites and other hazards.[3] Drinking rum and being in and around rum shop spaces offered the same communal and perhaps even therapeutic opportunities for men as they did for women. Since Black womanhood was already seen as a transgressive womanhood, some never even tried to fit the norms set out under other types of 'good womanhood'. Also, the society did not change much after legal emancipation; many women continued to work in agriculture and many conducted their lives without steady male partners – just like their foremothers had. This gender identity continued to grow and find form. Butch heterosexuality is a category of masculine femininity that is not helpless or supple or defined by its usefulness or proximity to patriarchy or men.

The fact that Butch het women sleep with men does not mean that they also give away their agency, love for a male aesthetic or desire to be alone or to determine their financial and economic agency. It is a gender performance a woman can use to express racial pride and resilience, a comfortable construction of herself as a Black woman and still like dick! – because isn't that what it means to be butch? To like what one likes and to be how one is comfortable despite the expectations set in place by the patriarchal/hetero-binary? Butch heterosexuality is not a woman trying to act like a man. But if Butch heterosexuality does not exist, is the suggestion that every heterosexual woman agrees to patriarchal subjugation and a gender order that says she is inferior to and not strong/er than men? Masculinity and femininity reside in every human being. Reconnecting to both as women leads us to more balanced and sustainable ways of being. Despite (Caribbean) Black womanhood showing up the flaws of the heteropatriarchal gender binary, the belief in the binary has stubbornly persisted. CC gender relations are now in a mire that offers no solutions due to these contradictions. Honest and open discussions about women's lived realities are needed. They must tackle the unmet and frankly unreasonable expectations of Caribbean men that women will continue to prop up a broken masculinity in exchange for heterosexual gratification. As Gregg cogently articulates,

> A focus on **gender** and its many guises would play a part in releasing us from the many layered prison house of contradictions that we now inhabit. Studying the mutual determinations of manhood and womanhood, and their interrelations, within the context of Caribbean history and knowledge systems would open up many new and rewarding areas and throw light on old problems (xvii).

Freeing ourselves of the Caribbean gender prison involves breaking fully free of a colonized notion of gender relations that envision women only in relationships with men as a priori subjugated. Gender identity should be fully constitutive without sexuality erasing it. Gender and sexuality are mutually exclusive and are only combined in cisgenderism. Cisgenderism is a possibility in a plethora of possibilities.

Butch heterosexuality is a gender philosophy/identity unveiled by Black womanhood that employs fluidity between characteristics traditionally marked as male and brings those into use by women if they are sensible in societal terms. It reconciles some of the challenges that are peculiar to Black female embodiment given the ruptures and racial embrace[4] of the Transatlantic experience. It is a reclamation of womanhood for Caribbean women beyond the cooptation of our womanhood to construct Caribbean manhood in a way that leaves us in a present absence (Gregg 2–4). I agree with Jack Halberstam that butchness should neither be conflated with transsexuality nor forced into the category of gender normativity (Halberstam 153–4). While Butch heterosexuals will run into the problem of not being butch enough compared to other classes such as stone butch or butch loving butch,[5] ask any butch Black woman trying to be in partnership with a Black man, and that woman has learnt that they are different and butch enough! Seek the issue that causes the perennial friction between Caribbean Black men and Caribbean Black women in gender relations, and they will tell you Caribbean women are too too aggressive, too mannish, too independent. From male complaints about the lack of a hairstyle (usually meaning Black women who wear natural hair or low hair styles), to the complaints about wearing pants every day, to the plea for heels, every Butch het woman knows that butchness is not about body (deviance) as much as it is about who has access to a woman's body and who does not have access – who gets upset and threatened when access is denied. If the urge to set up heteronormative/colonial binaries cannot be resisted then perhaps butch heterosexuality would be on one side of the spectrum – a kind of 'butch-lite', and stone butches perhaps would be the opposite end.

While my purpose in this book is not to argue that every Caribbean woman identifies with the gender identity Butch heterosexual, I do argue that there are women in the Caribbean who have always resisted masculine subjugation by themselves embodying masculinity. Women did not just resist subjugation because they were queer or lesbian. To conflate their resistance as only related to queer sexual orientation is to diminish their overall mission. In fact, resisting unsafety and subjugation was even a feature of other performances of womanhood, more dominant and more amenable to patriarchal hierarchical order. Jessica Marie Johnson, in *Wicked Flesh*, explores freedom, intimacy and kinship of Black women in relation to the experience of PPC. She asserts and I agree that plantation conditioned experiences of sex, gender relations and race and disconnected them from what pertained in Africa (8). She explores how transplanted African women negotiated what she calls 'Black femme freedom' (Johnson 10).

Although Johnson does not clearly describe what she means by Black femme performances of womanhood, she does make clear that these women used care and intimacy economies to secure their own freedom and agency in the encounter with colonialism (Johnson 14). I believe that the performance of womanhood that Johnson describes and the tactics used by women to link themselves to both white and Black men for the advantages is a feature of the dominant performance of womanhood in the CC. One of my major contentions in articulating Butch heterosexuality is that Black femme women, although they clearly rejected and redirected subjugation as Johnson shows, are read as less of a problem than women who see themselves as equal to men and who do not take the extra steps to make men comfortable in their daily negotiations of life. Black femme women found their status in connection with husbands or proximity to men (Johnson 18; 21). I think the kind of femininity that Hilary Beckles describes in *Natural Rebels* is more aligned with Black femme performances of womanhood, and I think it is a kind of womanhood – a dominant approach – which continued after legal emancipation and independence, but it is not the only approach to Black womanhood. It is also an approach to womanhood more in line with the Victorian notions of family that encouraged Black women to seek marriage and to serve their husbands as wives. Notwithstanding however, neither Black femme approaches to womanhood nor Butch heterosexuality are totally accepting of individualistic patriarchy. This means that Black men in the Caribbean have always built their expectations of manhood on non-existent dreams rather than anything existing in reality, as the discussion shows so far.

Black women in the CC live without men for various reasons. Some reasons were self-determined, steeped in refusal to be in unsafe relations characterized by domestic or other types of abuse, and others were due to the historical realities of capitalist bust and boom. Others were related to the boom-and-bust cycles of plantation economy. Men left for work, such as during the 1900s building of the Panama Canal years or during the 1950s and 1960s when immigration opportunities opened up in, for example, farm work programmes in North America (Richardson 123; Mohammed 41). Women also migrated in search of betterment. Despite the kind of womanhood Black Caribbean women subscribe to, independence has always been highly valued (51). Due to the intersectional connection between sexual autonomy and economic prosperity, many Black women, in whichever period of gender ratooning, were forced into positions where they did not have control over their bodies or sexuality. Many of them found themselves in relationships or arrangements with men who exchanged shelter and financial support for sexual relations and favours. Caribbean women understood that greater sexual freedom and autonomy were directly connected to being able to gain steady employment (Mohammed 51). Women in Barbados and the Caribbean, like their foremothers before them, opted not to get married to retain what autonomy and control they could over their lives. Caribbean women from generation to generation took care to instil in girls the importance of education and finding work to be able to navigate and negotiate relationships. The next section outlines how legal marriage and Victorian ideals of family undermined women's autonomy and some of their means of retaining control and protection of themselves and their children.

As in the case of understanding masculinity in Barbados and the CC after legal emancipation, independence and the contemporary society, two-handed reading is important to understand women and their performances of womanhood. Womanhood in the CC has been a contested space. From the cooptation of the emotional, sexual and physical labour of Black women by white masters on the plantation to the expectation of Black men that Black women would lean back and accept their dominion to the vilification of Black women as too strong, dysfunctional as mothers and generally brash and brazen, Black women have always had to defend their right to be and to exist and thrive.

State Mechanics, Women and Men

Veronica Gregg terms the mechanisms through which Black women were relegated beyond the boundaries of law and sin as 'constitutive negation' (8). In this section, I argue that constitutive negation is a colonial relic still characterizing the lives of Barbadian women. A 'fake personhood' is developed for Caribbean women characterized by "… fake autonomy [and] made to bear the burden of, and responsibility for, the treatment meted out to her by those who enforce the logic of the slave society" (8). This pattern of interaction can be clearly seen by examining the relations between the state, men and women in the family court system. There, the distance between men's perceptions about being marginalized and ill-treated by women and women's desires to maintain control over their lives and to cohabit in intimate partnerships that are safe and mutually beneficial play out. The state fails both parties in its maintenance of a PPC status quo, replicating a set of colonial logics harmful to both Black men and Black women.

Gregg explains that plantation logics were upheld by a tripartite web of legal, social and cultural connectors (26). Constitutive negation happens at important points in the first stage of making plantation, but there is also another important moment in the first gender ratooning. Women in plantation society were first constructively negated when their wombs were converted into tombs separating the humanized from the dehumanized – the free from the unfree. Motherhood on the plantation served an important labour function to PPC, but due to high instances of interracial sex, it also posed a potentially destabilizing effect. The Black womb became the subject of law that made its contents carry the status of the mother – that is to say that Blackness was created through matrilineality in PPC. I think this point solves a decades-old contention about whether the Caribbean society is matrilineal, matrifocal or patriarchal. It is an example of the often inextricable way that race and gender are intertwined (Morgan 2). Blackness in plantation society was matrilineal, but the plantation system was maintained and upheld by individualistic patriarchy and PPC. This is an example of the mess and contradictions inherent in plantation. The raced and gendered manipulation of the Black womb in PPC also bears out Gregg's hypothesis of constitutive negation. Black women were important to bear children that were branded as labour for plantation but in producing these 'non-human' wretched, they also further negated themselves in the racial enterprise. When Edward Long and others sought to make the children produced with Black women the sole responsibility of woman who could not lean on (often white) patrilineal inheritance and citizenship rights, women were again along for the ride to take sole responsibility for children almost as a trustee (overseeing their children's interests) but not in their own right as capable parent (25).

Women were negated because they had no power to name a father and hold him to account for his progeny. This mechanism, first important to ensuring the maintenance of white supremacy, lives on in the Caribbean as an important feature of individualistic patriarchy. The Bastardry Laws of the 1800s reinforced matrilineality and the constitutive negation of Black women in the juridical realm. Because Black women in the Caribbean have historically existed to please and serve others, the Bastardy Law is often read for its effects on children only, with its revocations being celebrated as a seminal moment in the creation of a better and more modern Caribbean society (Richardson 57; Thomas, *Exceptional Violence* 82). However, my contention is slightly different. While the replacement Bastardry Law with more favourable legislation, such as the Minors Act (1891 in Barbados) and the Status of Children Act (1979 in Barbados), was beneficial for children, it did not fix the issue of constitutive negation in the lives of mothers. Matrilineality was also discontinued altogether in Barbados with the passage of the Minors Act, CAP 215. Section four of CAP 215 gave joint custody to both parents of a child. Again, a two-handed approach is necessary to understand the nuance I am trying to highlight. Through legislation, social and cultural values, plantation motherhood first rendered Black women the bearers of the dehumanized category – slave. Then, mothers of miscegenated offspring were silenced from naming their rapists, masters and consorts through a law forbidding inheritance rights for their children. The next formation sought to relieve the state of financial responsibility for absent fathers which had become a feature in the CC for varying reasons. In all those formations, matrilineality was a mechanism used by the state to manipulate the Black womb. None of these formations was about embodying Black women or their right to carry children, and in the contemporary moment, laws to protect children are now being used to keep women in present absence in family matters before the court.

When matrilineality was no longer needed by white men in PPC and it served Black men who wanted dominion over women and children as true patriarchs, the law (Minor's Act) made the product of the Black womb equal parts the mother's and the father's. None of these constellations has respected or revered the right of the Black woman to parent. Constitutive negation of women as autonomous people and parents started on plantation and continued into first and second gender ratoons. Despite the age-old assertion that the Black mother is sacred in Caribbean society I again find myself in agreement with Gregg that watching both what is said and done is critical (28). Even in the realm of motherhood, where a woman is seen at her most biologically vulnerable, Black women were forced to fight and defend autonomy (Sheller 54–9). Given the contradictions and complexities of plantation society, the CC is a maze of points and counterpoints – full understanding requires knowledge and appreciation of the nuance. There is no vulnerable, supplicant posture inbuilt in Black womanhood. Strength, resiliency and the ability to defend self and the offspring on the plantation battlefield were and are important life skills for Black women. If they are relentlessly strong, it is because their environment demands it. In the final section of this chapter, I lay out the life profile of a woman to show how constitutive negation continues as a contemporary issue in PPC. The issues I try to outline in this book are not abstract. They are the issues that still affect the lives of women in the CC at alarming rates.

A Case Study

Maude was born in a neighbouring Caribbean Island. When she was two her mother left her in the care of sisters and migrated to Barbados.[6] Her mother then sent for Maude and brought her to Barbados as a tender-aged child of five or six. Maude reported that her mother did not like her father and she believes her mother took out the rage meant for her father on her. In Barbados, Maude lived with her mother and her mother's partner. Her mother's partner was abusive. He beat Maude's mother and put her out of the house. When Maude was nine, her mother was deported. Maude's mother, left alone; she believed that Maude stood a better chance staying in Barbados. However, things did not go as Maude's mother hoped. Her mother's deportation started cycles of family instability. Her mother's partner neglected to provide food, and many days Maude went to school hungry. In addition, Maude had to use the community pipe for baths. She recounts an old neighbour watching her bathe one day. He asked her where her mother was and she responded that her mother was not there. The neighbour told her she looked hungry and offered her some food. She remembers when she went to his house, while he fed her the food with one hand he performed finger sex on her with the other. Maude's mother's partner had a simultaneous relationship with the mother of his children. There has been friction and fighting between the two women when Maude's mother had been in Barbados. However, the man took Maude to his children's mother.

Not surprisingly, that arrangement did not last long. Maude bounced between households for a few months before ending up with Sally – a friend of her mother's. Sally lived with her partner, and Maude reported that she was put on the floor of the couple's room to sleep. It was not long before

Sally's partner would leave his bed and come to the floor to have sex with Maude. Maude said she was hungry, and she took the abuse without complaining because she was hungry. After a few months a lady visited the home. She had one son and asked if she could take Maude to be company for her son. Maude said the house was modest but it was the safest she felt as a child. Maude's mother returned to the Island at this point and learn of her whereabouts. Her new family pleaded with her mother to let her stay but her mother was not amenable. Maude then moved to the same home her mother had been deported from with the man who had abandoned her. Shortly after they returned to the house, the man's grown son moved in with his father. Maude's mother allowed the man to share a bed with Maude and she was sexually abused by her older stepbrother. Maude explained that if her mother started a new relationship and the partner wanted to sleep with her, her mother allowed it as long as they were fed and kept in shelter. She changed schools according to where her mother's latest partner lived. Maude has lived in all eleven parishes of Barbados.

Maude recounts an experience of living in St. Philip with one of her mother's partners. When her mother left her home sick one day, the man returned home. Maude did not let him into the house because her mother was not there. The man complained to her mother that Maude was rude. Maude's mother beat her and told her that she had been rude to the man, who only wanted to be 'a father figure'. In another instance, Maude recounts that there was another time when her mother moved in with a man on the south of the island. She explains:

> My mother moved me into the house with this man. The first thing he did was paint the windows black. He worked at the M[inistry of] T[ransport and] W[orks]. The Black paint they worked with to paint the roads, he used to paint the windows. When I came home and wanted to go out to play with my friends, that was a problem. If I go to the store and he looks out and sees anyone talking to me, problem. One day my mother went to work. I had migraine headaches as a teenager. I could not look at bright lights and the headaches were so severe they would put me to sleep. This particular Saturday, I was in bed with a headache and in between sleep and wake I felt a weight over me. I started to fight but I was not strong enough. I had a dislike for this man. I do not hate people but I hated him. Some how, I fought him off of me. I ran to our outside bathroom and I started to bath and scrub. He ran after me and made me watch him masturbate until he ejaculated.

Maude's school performance started to falter. Her teachers at school made an appointment for her at the health clinic. She saw a psychiatrist but when what she had reported to the authorities was relayed to her mother she was beaten for having reported her experiences. When Maude started to fend off her mother's partner's sexual come-ons he told her mother she had to leave.

Maude's mother arranged for her to be taken in by a woman friend. That woman friend invited men to visit the house to have sex with Maude for money. She remembers:

> There was one. He was a food and beverage manager at a hotel. He came to see one me one night. Soon after the woman I lived with told me to go and get ready. I asked her get ready for what? She said Mr. X was coming to carry me out. I was about fourteen/fifteen. As soon as I got into the car I told him my age. I told him I do not know what he was told but I was only a child. He took me to a popular party spot and then he took me home. My mother's friend was livid when I got home. I guess he told her what I had been saying. She beat me that night and the next night the man came back. She ordered me to shower and go with him. The man took me to a popular beach where couples parked to have sex. I have never had sex so hard – nobody has ever screwed me so hard before or since.
>
> Days later she took me to another man's house. We were all talking and I did not even realize when she left me. Shortly after the man held a gun to my head and raped me.

The two incidents left Maude with abdominal pains. Maude went to school one day and she just went into a daze and walked away from the school. This incident triggered authorities to move her to a children's home. Maude was suicidal. Maude remembers leaving the children home one day and catching the bus to school. Her stomach started hurting on the bus and when she got up to get off the bus the conductor told her she had blood on her clothes and directed her back into her seat. The bus took her directly to her school. The school gave Maude sanitary ware and sent her back to the children's home. She remembers barely getting there when she had a pain that rendered her motionless. She said the pain was followed by a series of clots. When the doctor was summoned, he told Maude that she had had a spontaneous abortion. Maude remembers that the treatment at the children's home was mixed. Maude explained that some of the aunties in the home were very supportive and others were not. Some aunties read the file and then used the information as the base of insults. Maude recalls having to go to counselling at the childcare agency in Barbados. She explains that the officer in charge of the counselling started to make her wait until last for her sessions. He propositioned her several times. He told her he could take care of her and provide for her if they had a 'special relationship'. While Maude did not give in to the propositions, she says she stopped looking into the mirror completely. For years she struggled with feelings of dirtiness and self-disdain. As Maude got older and tried to discuss the abuse, her mother has consistently denied that the abuse happened although her mother did receive, on Maude's behalf, a financial settlement in relation to the two incidents of abuse that led to her miscarriage.

Maude met Paul after a series of abusive relationships with men. She was looking for love and not being successful. When Maude ran from the last abusive relationship she moved back in with her mother and two young sons. The relationship between her and her mother was quite strained. When Maude met Paul, she was intrigued that a man wanted to talk to her after all she had been through. His booming voice helped the situation. Maude believes she fell for Paul because she chose him and it was a romance she had never had to that point. Shortly after the relationship began to blossom, Maude realized that patterns of dysfunction were also present in Paul's family. Paul has a severe gambling addiction – Maude has seen him and his father gamble together. Like Maude, Paul received severe beatings in childhood. Paul confided in Maude that he never felt loved in his childhood family unit. The couple got married less than a year after meeting. In reflecting on their relationship dynamic, Maude, who is older than Paul, explains that she thinks Paul was seeking a mother figure more than a partner in getting together with her.

Maude was the breadwinner for much of the relationship. While Paul liked the fruits of Maude's industriousness, her being away from home to work also created jealousy. When she dressed for work or spoke standard English, she was accused of trying to be better than Paul. Maude's financial security at the beginning of the union threatened Paul. Maude has a vast contact base in Barbados due to her career in tourism. Paul has benefited from the network, such as when Maude brokered what was Paul's first stable job outside of the home. Despite the benefits, Paul was resentful of the network and constantly accused Maude of infidelity. When Paul lost his job due to poor attendance, Maude developed and financed business initiatives for Paul. When Maude went overseas to work, she bought lingerie for Paul to sell. She reports that although the stock was depleted, money was never made. Another business venture included financing a taxi for Paul. Paul wrote the taxi off, collected the insurance payout and kept the payout, while Maude is left to pay the loan on the vehicle. Maude and Paul settled on his family's land located in a rural tenantry in Barbados. Since the titles to tenantry land are usually not clear, financial institutions do not take them as collateral. To improve the house that Maude moved into with Paul she used her mother's property to secure a renovation loan. Maude was able to build a three-bedroom family house and furnish it. This is the house she ran and left to get herself and her children away from Paul's physical abuse. Paul remains in the house but refuses to take over the loan. Maude is paying the loan because she does not want her mother to lose her home. Maude also pays to rent the apartment she shares with her children.

The children have grown up seeing Maude being beaten by their father. Although she has left the union, both children are affected. The daughter, who is sixteen, bed-wets and her son, fourteen, has nightmares and cannot go back to bed unless he is next to his mother. He tells her that he dreams that daddy was beating her and he just wants to be next to her to ensure she is safe. Maude's son is also struggling with anger and got into an altercation at school.

Both children have decided that they no longer want to pursue an active relationship with their father. This triggered the family court judge presiding over the access and maintenance case in court to chastise Maude for turning the children against their father. The judge threatened to make Maude's children wards of the court to enforce visitation. Meanwhile, the financial abuse that Maude is facing while being before the court is not being considered. An order for maintenance of the children was made by the court but Paul refuses to pay. A further order for garnishment had to be made, but due to backlogs in court administration, the order is yet to be enacted. Meanwhile the financial burden is taking a toll on Maude and her credit is ruined.

Maude struggles to provide support for her children even as she experiences severe headaches, tiredness and neck pains. Neither Maude nor her children are in counselling. Free access to counselling services through the psychiatric community mental health programme is inundated. The Family Service Division of the Welfare Department, the state agency charged with supporting families in need of intervention, declined to do another report on the family when the judge requested it. Maude says the way she is treated in court is almost as bad as being beaten by Paul. She struggles to understand why she was never protected by the system, neither as a child nor now as a survivor of intimate partner violence.

Maude ends her interview by telling me in a quiet but defiant voice, "It ended with me. The cycle ended with me. My daughter is sixteen and she is intact. It ended with me".

The cycle of sexual abuse ends with Maude because she stood in the breach for her children. Whether the damage of living with an abusive father negatively skews her daughter's choices of intimate partner is left to be seen. Whether the system in Barbados is better able to offer an intervention if Maude's daughter finds herself in an abusive relationship are all things Maude cannot control as hard as she has tried – such is life on a plantation. The concerns outlined in the case study of Maude mirror those in Suzanne LaFont's study of gender relations in family court in Jamaica (LaFont 26; 57; 67–8). I contend that the experiences of Maude are not unique or extreme. They mirror some of the personal testimonies of women I have worked with over time. They mirror my own lived experience. I, too, was offered a special relationship for my care when I tried to get intervention from the same childcare authorities in Barbados. Testimonies of former wards held in The Government Industrial School, a residential school still operational, reveal that many of them were either offered or forced into such arrangements. Although I fled my abuser's house when I was sixteen years old, he stole an inheritance meant for me by forging my grandmother's and my signature.

To this day as I write this book, although I have a judgement for the money stolen to be repaid, like Paul, my abuser refuses to honour the court agreement and given the constitutive negation that shapes womanhood in the court, nothing is done. Maude's case represents the unresolved issues of how Black womanhood is constructed in Barbados and the court is complicit in upholding status quo. Many Barbadian women have court orders for maintenance or divorce settlements that are never enforced by the court. Resultingly Barbadian women live in gendered poverty – punishment for daring to be strong enough to leave abusers and feel they should be able to go on with their lives as full embodied citizens with access to their own financial and emotional resources. The stories in *Lion Heart Gyal* reveal that Maude's issues replicate across the Caribbean. The work of women scholars, inter alia, *Women's Untold Stories*, *Surviving the Silence* and *Longing to Tell* reveals that Maude's story is a colonial relic – a manifestation of present absence arising from the way Black womanhood was constructed and continues to be perceived in a racially/gendered stratified world.

Black CC women are expected to uplift their children and their men. Their safety is dispensable and, as has always been the case on Caribbean plantations, their motherhood and right to parent are constantly being questioned and manipulated for the benefit of someone else. Independence and the nationalist project did not resolve these issues, rather independence resulted in nationalism and individualistic patriarchy becoming fused. It is in this context that masculine femininity and the effort to delink from patriarchal manipulation are misunderstood. It continues to ferment in the Caribbean context. If Maude had not been a strong, resilient woman, the stress and despair of her situation might have knocked her over. Time and time again she has turned scars into triumph. She is a strong woman because the dysfunction of plantation legitimated by the judiciary and broader social services system demands it. The only way to resist constitutive negation is to boldly and unapologetically take up space – not just as a mother but as a human deserving of dignity, respect and the right to thrive.

Conclusion

In Chapter 1, I noted a similarity between individualistic patriarchy and butch heterosexuality. A major feature of both is unfettered personal freedom. However, a major difference between individualistic patriarchy and Butch heterosexuality is that the former is a dominant gender identity, and the latter is a stigmatized and undesirable masculine-feminine identity. Where individualistic patriarchy is seen as a desirable performance of manhood and upheld via PPC status quo, as desirable masculinity and manhood, Butch heterosexuality is seen as an out-of-place and troublesome masculine femininity. Another major difference between the two identities is that Butch heterosexuality is an anti-colonial, gender expansive, liberatory tactic grounded in survival. Individualistic patriarchy is colonial, gender rigid and detrimentally excessive. Butch heterosexuality is turned inward and is a personal strategy of survival, while individualistic patriarchy demands the

Table 2.1 The features of Plantocratic Patriarchal Culture

PPC man – Individual level	*PPC woman – Individual level*	*PPC – State level*
Men expect control over and benefits of women's emotional and sexual labour without any accountability for the safety and protection of women.	Women are controlled by high level of respectability that controls their sexuality and rewards them for being loyal to individualistic patriarchs.	Subjugation of women, queer, disabled and other vulnerable groups in society because they are seen as needing guidance and direction.
Men expect to be upheld as heads of the household and to dominate space in the public sphere, including the top jobs in political and governmental leadership.	Women are expected to support the male marginalization position and not to assert themselves beyond being wives and mothers.	State mechanisms that uphold the control of subjugated populations.
Men are not accountable for care of subjugated groups including women, children, the elderly or disabled. While they expect to exert control, especially over women and children, they reject being financially responsible for these groups.	Women are expected to uphold the PPC status quo and women who are not are labelled as dangerous, radical or man-hating.	A civil service and governmental functions that seem to support the care of subjugated populations but that actually perpetuate the PPC status quo and do harm to subjugated populations.

subjugation of others and the use of state and governmental resources to uphold individual egos and privilege – one can survive and remain relevant in a contemporary world, the other is wholly outdated. PPC uplifts men, but it also implicates women and is legitimated by the state. Table 2.1 shows the overarching effects.

PPC gives rise to severe violence and dysfunction in familial relationships. The dysfunction in Barbados and the CC is a direct relic of the experience of slavery and its afterlives. Generally thinkers either study the family or governance and politics. However, the family is inextricably affected by the society in which it lives. Through the sections of this chapter, I hope I showed how PPC affects the family and also how the status quo reinforces PPC. The toxic features of individualistic patriarchy were embedded into the nationalist project of the Caribbean, and they create an expectation that Black women will serve as mothers and wives without any protection or benefits of their own. So is the state of gender relations in Barbados and the CC. In Chapter 3 I suggest what I believe an intervention could look like.

Notes

1 See bell hooks' analysis of the effects of patriarchy on the beliefs of Black men and Black family life in *Salvation: Black people and Love* (156–7).

2 Veronica Gregg makes a fundamental point when she explains that Caribbean women are divided by race, class and orientations with "irreconcilable conflicts and differences" (Gregg xiv). Studies on the tensions and contentions between different types of Caribbean women are, I would suggest, an understudied and critical area of study.

3 Glory Robertson explains that wearing men's clothing was frowned upon in nineteenth-century Jamaica (115). Robertson's analysis seems to focus on middle- and upper-class women. Black women who worked in agriculture in Barbados wore trousers and men's shirts for their protection and freedom of movement. I saw my grandmother and several other women in her age group wearing man clothing to work in the fields and to tend their animals. The pictures in Robertson's articles still show that working women dressed very differently to their middle- and upper-class peers of leisure (112; 114).

4 I borrow this term from Phanuel Antwi's essay on the "Racial Embrace" (27–36).

5 Halberstam explains that stone butches and butch loving butches are seen as 'extremes'. He explains that they are often defined in limited and negated ways (118–26).

6 See Mohammed (54–6) for more on inter-island migration trends.

3 Butch Heterosexuality

Black Women Are (Gender) Innovators

Although Black Commonwealth Caribbean (CC) women have not been credited as innovators, they disproportionately built modernity on their backs and in their bellies. Others have gotten rich off our tears and our stolen dreams. Black Caribbean women deserve society in which their dreams can be reclaimed – where our sexual exploitation and harm stop. The CC has work to do not just in homes but in the governance project and wider society. The last two chapters outlined the historical and contemporary gender map in the Caribbean. In this chapter I want to begin postulating about the future. I see the future as inclusive and while I think through heterosexual relations in Barbados and the CC it is high time that respect is given to other types of love as well. It is as much a harmful colonial relic that queer people in the CC have to hide their relations as it is for heterosexual relations to be governed by individualistic patriarchal gender norms. Plantation logics demand that some citizens are deemed more deserving of protection, resources and access to citizenship rights than others.[1] What is the future? What is a society in which Butch heterosexuality can thrive as a legitimate, non-threatened and non-threatening performance of womanhood? Section "Reconciling Race" sets out some of the behaviours and practices that still plague Caribbean societies and the gender tensions that must be negotiated to create such a society.

Section "Black, Trauma-Informed Partnership" takes liberation to ground zero – the site where a Black woman and man meet and try to form their lives into a union. I suggest general features of mutually healthy and supportive partnerships beyond patriarchal formations. Section "Rethinking Gender Justice and Theory" offers a reconceptualization of gender theory that eschews feminism, like many women in the Caribbean do and advocates for womanism as a theoretical space that can underpin the intimate changes between Black men and Black women. Feminism has not been a useful construct for women in the CC and they have not resonated with it as a body politic. Gender justice requires a gender theory that supports justice as a principle. I offer a 'new' womanism that can flow from a personal project of reframing gender relations to a broader social project. The final section, "Rethinking the State: Nationalism Reclaimed" encourages people in the Caribbean to step back into

DOI: 10.4324/9781003518709-4

the methods and intellectual spaces of the 1930s and 1960s to reclaim our liberation movement. A part of that must be creating an unequivocal place for the concerns of women in Barbados and addressing constitutive negation as a contemporary reality.

At the moment the PPC status quo offers women very few options to tap into patriarchal privilege/fit into a deserving group. One has to be seen as a good mother, professional man, able-bodied worker and invest in upholding the category by leveraging it against people deemed different to uphold their position. Thus, poor people, dark or disabled people are the opposite of the privileged classes – bad mother, skilled worker, disabled person. PPC is concentrated because along with the stratification based on a person's usefulness to economic activity is also the social contract that Carol Pateman highlights. According to her, the classical contract that creates all societies, including plantation society, is upheld by a double contract that legitimate political and governmental power on the one hand and the subjugation of women (through marriage/heterosexual relations) on the other (Pateman 4). Heterosexuality, instead of simply being a biological descriptor for sex between people with different chromosomal markers, becomes a moniker for subjugation. Gender performances that claim masculinity beyond maleness can challenge the sexual contract that created and legitimate patriarchy and that is why strong women are seen as so problematic.

Reconciling Race

Much damage has been done to Black women, men, children and families through upholding individualistic patriarchy. There is no way to move the CC forward without a new set of contractual arrangements that supplant those underpinning plantation society. Deborah Thomas in *Exceptional Violence* cogently argues that the state of violence and dysfunction in contemporary CC societies is not accidental or new. Like Thomas and others, I believe that reparative justice offers a sensible framework to think and work through severing some of the most deeply rooted and harmful aspects of colonial logics and relics (DeGruy 12–13; Thomas, *Exceptional Violence* 174–5). I hasten to add that reparations through the mechanism of the CARICOM ten-point plan is not the kind of reparative justice I am endorsing. Thomas notes that two of the most useful potential remedies of reparations in the CC are underlining the way that racialization affects citizenship and citizenship rights and the space to call out class relations and the inherent problems of class in the CC (DeGruy 12–13; Thomas, *Exceptional Violence* 174–5). The current structure of the CARICOM ten-point plan does not allow for those two critical correctives. Firstly, the plan is completely outward-looking. Although the plan acknowledges that Western colonization remains a continuous feature in upholding the geographic divide between the global north and the global south, it is written as though the damage done is largely historical (preamble).

The effects of plantation are ongoing and the very class responsible for the betrayal of the Caribbean independence and nationalist movement – the CC intellectual and middle class – is the very class in control of the ten-point reparations plan. Resultingly, the same kind of ideological contradictions that undermine the nationalist project itself and cause implementation deficit in Caribbean social justice projects replicate in the CARICOM ten-point plan. The CC politourgeoise, intellectuals and middle class uphold plantation and are agents of colonialism and neo-colonialism. They have as much of an apology and adjustment to make in relation to their treatment of other classes of Barbadians and citizens of the CC as the historical oppressors.

Secondly, CARICOM's ten-point plan does not address the internal racial tensions in Barbados and the CC. Relations between the white and Black populations of the Caribbean are fraught. Colourism based on shade of skin and grade of hair is not an issue that will be resolved with the largesse of the international world. Racism is as much an internal problem as an external one. It was never just a problem of how others in the world treat us but also a problem of how Caribbean people treat each other and ourselves. Even if reparations yield maximal redress the world is willing to offer, and the proceeds are brought back to a region where individualist capitalists believe they can appropriate the resources for their gain, women and children are still left unfree. The women of the CC should no longer be expected to throw their efforts into nation-building and expect that their needs will be met after the nation is built. That was the approach to independence and nationalism – even revolution and it has failed (Andaiye 42–4). Thus, third and relatedly, there is not one action item in the ten-point plan that addresses gender relations in the CC. Racial capitalism is set up with race and gender as two sides of the same coin and as I have argued to this point these relations have been hindering the citizenship experiences of both men and women.

I encourage research projects that document and trace other female masculinities and their historical moorings. Notwithstanding, I believe that Butch heterosexuality is a unique kind of gender performance of womanhood grounded in the historical experiences of Black women in the Atlantic World. Far from being a pathology or reactive approach to plantation, it was a way that Black women orchestrated and designed their gender performances to survive constitutive negation. To avoid an ideological quagmire negotiating race – which is not biological but which at the same time has resulted in certain gender performances based on the experiences of socially constituted race – a two-handed approach to conceptualize race is useful. Plantation race logics still generates social abandonment and mistreatment for large portions of CC population, including women, children, the elderly, the poor, disabled, queer and mad. As Thomas argues, neoliberalism creates "stateless and illegitimate [people] stripped of all claims to political or social citizenship, not unlike those slaves [SIC] on New World plantations" (Thomas, *Exceptional Violence* 44).

To possess a birth certificate in the Caribbean is not to possess full embodiment as a citizen. It is not to have enough land to occupy adequate space as a family or with a family. Large tracks of land in Barbados are still owned by absentee landlords, and other tracks are actively being sold to foreign investors. In the dying days of 2023, Barbados learnt that taxpayer dollars were to be used to purchase the famous Drax Hall Plantation.[2] Despite the CARICOM ten-point plan, the neoliberal acolyte and Prime Minister of Barbados was willing to enrich an already rich plantation dynasty without a real or enduring plan for the land to be acquired. The government did eventually renege on its plan but then the people of Barbados discovered that the landing site of the first English settlers to the Island, and one of the last public beach access points in Holetown, was sold to a Canadian land developer at peppercorn. While the government of Canada is negotiating a process of reconciliation with the Indigenous populations across Canada, one of the primary goals of which is to keep alive the question of unceded land and returning it to the Indigenous populations, neoliberal businessmen are in bed with the Barbadian politourgeoise and divvying up Barbados as if it were frontier (Thomas, *Exceptional Violence* 44). Public land at the famous Bathsheba and Teacup and Saucer picnic areas have all been sold to foreign investors. All this as Barbadians and CC people more broadly fight to retain their pride and connection to land (Beckles, *Chattel House Blues Making of a Democratic Society in Barbados* 145, Patterson 216–20, Richardson 58). The earth is gendered female. She is seen as a supplicant and for the taking and making of man and wealth. There can be no reconciliation for race relations in Barbados and the CC if the land resources continue to be beyond the use of Black Barbadians.

The struggle that Black men in Barbados have then is not with the women of Barbados. The women of Barbados have not taken power from Black Barbadian men. Our education and desire to be autonomous are not a threat to Black masculinity. The threat to Black masculinity is in the continual collaboration between the politourgeoise and foreign neoliberal investors to dispossess Barbadian men of their reparative and birthright justice. Chika Onyeani asserts in his frank account of Blackness that the Black race has remained slaves because it consumes more than it produces (5). Related to the imbalance between consumption and production is the sale of land in the CC. Capitalism has made us commodify something that our ancestors understood as far more. Land for CC ancestors was a means to produce food but also craft and other items that could be sold. Land created the basis of familial wealth and was the beginning of respect and dignity. In reconciling race, the Black men of Barbados must demand that the politourgeoise stop selling and in some case giving away[3] land in Barbados.

While I have time for Chika Onyeani's general call to action about being mindful consumers and businesspeople to enhance the global position of the Black race, I fundamentally disagree that trying to be better capitalists than other races or kinds of capitalists is a serious solution. I also call out the fact that, like so many Black men before him, Onyeani's version of freedom only envisions a place for Black women in a support role (where they are likely to nag and hinder their men) rather than them being co-conspirators or leaders of freedom movements (Onyeani 22–3). Any new liberation strategy for the Black community has to treat race and gender as two unequivocally connected sides of the same colonial coin. Any movement that supports race liberation or reparative justice unwilling to consider the unique position of Black women are ones not worth fighting for or joining by Black women. Black men must be willing to fight for Black women in the same way that Black women must be willing to fight for Black men. Both must understand and recognize that any other configuration is a part of the colonial design to weaken us as a people and as family units (Patterson xlvi).

There can and should be no national agenda in Barbados or any Caribbean territory that is unwilling to reconcile gender issues, not as an appendage or concession granted to a few 'miserable women' but as required activity in the decolonization project of the region. Women in the Caribbean have tried to get their concerns on nationalist agenda, and I will not suggest that the creation of bureaus of gender affairs and other successes such as the Henry Forde-led commission on the Status of Women in Barbados and subsequent legalization including the abortion act were not successes. What I am contending is that women had to always be in a supple and comforting position to secure these successes. The issue of women in the Caribbean should not only be left to women elected to politics in traditional political parties. Many of these women have to make pacts with the men and masculine ideologies of the party to win electoral victories (Ellis 51; 57; 62). I do not agree with Patricia Eliss in her summation that being non-threatening in addressing gender issues has been a useful strategy (Ellis 76–7). What has happened is that diplomacy has been used to keep women in the Caribbean in check and to reinforce the belief that good women are not loud or 'aggressive'. The double standards required to agitate for a better set of gender norms in the Caribbean and operate within the parameters set by men have diluted the overall success of the women's movement (Ellis 84; 88; 94).

The current political process in the Caribbean is not working for the reconciliation of gender relations, or race relations for that matter. Contrary to popular belief, there are no hard and soft political issues. As I outlined above, there is a tangible correlation between the way that women are treated and the way that the environment is treated. Also as long as Caribbean culture is read in a disconnected way from the African culture that informs it, answers to the biggest questions will be elusive (DeGruy 18). For capitalism to work, there must always be free and cheap labour. Disproportionately, women provide care labour which is left out of the economic equation altogether. The systems that value men's labour while devaluing women's is replicated in how the earth is treated. Although taking from the earth is essential to human survival, it should be done in ways that honour and care but that is not what happens.

The political system in the Caribbean did not rupture racial/capitalist values at independence. As Jemima Pierre argues, "…postcolony…realities are connected to an interlinked set of practices, experiences and **belief systems** – a specific predicament of the long history of European empire making" (xii). Pierre's area of study is Ghana – a predominantly Black African country. The argument applies to the Caribbean aptly as the common denominator is the Transatlantic slave trade and the experience of colonialism. Pierre contends that postcolonial societies have "various sites through which racial meanings are crafted [and] racialization…deployed and articulated" (2). Politics, specifically charismatic leadership and the political strong men created by charisma, is a site of continued reproduction of racial meaning in the Caribbean. The white individualist patriarchs who built the political system in Barbados and the CC did not envision women's involvement. Nationalist leaders like Errol Barrow did not challenge those logics – they recrafted them from the purview of white men to the purview of Black men (41). Women's places in the CC have to be reshaped at the national and governmental level as well as within individual homes and intimate relations. According to the last census report, 52 percent of Barbados population selected the category of female to describe themselves. Yet, there is still national policy being made by less than half of the population for the rest of the population. Whether those decisions are made by men or by the surrogate women they strategically place in positions to protect their interest while ticking the 'gender representation box', the point is that the majority of Barbadian women are left on the outside of government, governance and policy.

If the women are largely left out of citizenship rights to participatory engagement then, why do the men of the Caribbean believe that the women are the ones who are subjugating them and stealing their ability to be men? It is because men in Barbados are subjugated by the politourgeoise – a small group of individuals who have coopted the independence movement of the Caribbean and refined it using politics to trick, sideline and frustrate the decolonizing process. Many of these people utilize national politics to secure wealth through nefarious deals with neoliberal, foreign businesses and businessmen, but they also manipulate other political processes, including the boards of grassroots organizations like credit unions, workers unions and volunteer organizations. Their interest is in securing prestige and amassing wealth just as owners of plantations were. They frustrate electoral processes and people who wish to see real change in the plantation structure of Barbadian society. The politourgeoise does not serve Black men in the Caribbean and it does not serve Black women. Black women and Black men should unite to reclaim the struggle for liberation. Women should assist men in organizing true liberation for Black men in the economic sphere and men should unite to ensure that women can move from their lot in constitutive negation in judicial and other social systems. Replicating this ideological unification of Black men and women should be the basis of individual heterosexual partnership formation. There can be no stronger or better family unity in the CC without addressing the political/systemic issues and how both Black men and women are being treated by the state.

Black, Trauma-Informed Partnership

My granny had a saying – two dry cows cannot make milk. Usually, her interpretation was a financial one. It was to remind us, as girls in the family that in seeking a romantic partner the choice should be designed to support 'setting up house' (i.e. buying a house and maintaining a family financially). Simultaneously with this reminder, though and far more often, granny reminded us as girls the importance of women being self-sufficient and not depending on a partner to be able to stand financially. Granny's cow adage became important to me as a guide for choosing an emotionally present partner. The sum total of a partnership is the individual elements of wellness of the partners. What does having a healthy partnership look like, given Joy Degruy's assertion that Black people "have experienced a legacy of trauma" (101). Having healthy partnerships in the Black community is an act best guided by two-handed approaches. At one and the same time a couple must accept the work of modern research on trauma and stress and how it affects individuals and communities affected by genocides such Transatlantic slavery and be open and willing to fix the consequences of that at the individual level and also work to provide their partner with the understanding and grace they need to thrive and live in a low-stress, supportive environment (Conti 11; DeGruy 18; Van Der Kolk 151–4). Black people are affected by trauma racially, generationally and individually. Our fight as Black men and Black women is not against each other but against historical experiences and how to unify in a partnership that is not based on subjugation, harm and usury.

Alternative gender expressions that push beyond notions of binary poles that women and men occupy open space for other conceptualizations of heterosexual relationships. I cannot change the biological wiring that results in my attraction to the other sex any more than a queer friend can change theirs to the same sex. What can change is our rearing of Black heterosexual boys which connects opposite sex desire to them having a right to domination and harmful relationship practices. As bell hooks notes pushing for different approaches to masculinity beyond patriarchal relations not only benefits patriarchal love, it makes for stronger relations between brothers, neighbours, colleagues and bosses and friends (hooks, *The Will to Change* 1–2). Black boys and girls should be taught the legacies of colonialism and how they give rise to gender trauma (Iantaffi 53–8). Although Alex Iantaffi theorizes based on Indigenous and trans experiences in explaining what they term gender trauma, the Black community is also significantly affected because gender differentiation and separation as an enduring colonial logic.

I agree with bell hooks that feminism failed to offer any kind of real solution to the colonial wound to be healed between Black men and Black women (hooks, *The Will to Change* xii). Feminism failed to provide the intellectual impetus necessary to understand (alternative) Caribbean womanhood. Equally important to declare is that individualistic patriarchy has abysmally disappointed in creating a framework of manhood. Black (Caribbean) men declare loudly about the failures of feminism but they hold steadfastly to Victorianism – both are external, foreign constructs that have failed us in our gender relations. In place of relationships, characterized by gender difference and different roles where women have no access to masculinity, the goal is to strive for trauma-informed partnership in rebuilding healthier relations between Black men and Black women. I think trauma-informed approaches have been effective in addressing what was traditionally labelled as dysfunctional or pathological (see Table 3.1).

Table 3.1 Components of Trauma-Informed Relationships for Black (Butch) heterosexual people

Trauma-informed mechanism	*Description*
A complete commitment to irradiate silence	A willingness to discuss frankly what Black femininity and masculinity are and how the partnership can bloom beyond the limitations of historical patterns. A willingness not to use silence to hide family issues or to walk away from difficult conversations. Ending silence is a willingness to change and to be individually responsible for change.
Trauma-informed therapy, individually and as a couple	The couple is only as strong as the weakest partner. Thus, each individual must be prepared to engage their own healing while also understanding the trauma of their partner and seeing their responsibility as holding safe space for their partner. The cost of trauma-informed care should be met out of the effort for reparative justice in the Caribbean as it is costly and beyond the means of many who need it the most.
Adequate rest and nutrition	A partnership does not begin on the day two people meet each other. It begins with their ability to feel like a whole and valued individual. Poverty, a lack of access to affordable housing and strong and stable primary family units all affect partnership success. People who are nutrient and sleep deprived are more likely to have harmful coping mechanisms like addiction or disassociation. Having to work multiple jobs cuts into family and partnership time. In developing CC economic policy, these issues must be on the table as important and not 'soft or women's issues'. Families do not thrive best under capitalist economic systems.

(*Continued*)

Table 3.1 (Continued)

Trauma-informed mechanism	*Description*
Commitment to stewardship of the future generation	Prevailing plantation logics are producing Caribbean dysfunction. Adverse Childhood Experiences (ACEs) produce adults that are ill-prepared to process life and meet challenges with resilience. Our history reveals the issues to be fixed as a people. Change requires a commitment to doing better if not for this generation for the next. It is not impossible to stop generational and racial trauma. Educational institutions are a major assets in the work to be done. The work of the nationalist era to revise curricula in history, language, geography and literature needs to be expanded. Content on trauma, gender and Black resilience content should be added.
No unequal power relations	Space for each individual in the relationship to be fluid between their masculine and feminine energies as is the natural human approach to life. Both men and women in partnership need a different view of what togetherness is and what it takes to be happy in partnership. Black couples can only get the partnership they work for and that is 100 percent a shared responsibility.
Community norms that encourage trauma-informed relationships	Individual couples in Barbados cannot dig their way out of the harms and unsafety affecting families. All stakeholders have to recognize the interlocked synergies between changing the overall social culture in Barbados and the CC, the functioning of the judiciary in relation to women and family law and gender and reparative justice. If couples practising trauma-informed partnership building receive patriarchal approaches to issues they may need to take before the court or other social services their efforts are lost in a systemic unsafety in relation to coupling.

Trauma-informed approaches are people-centred approaches. They replace the belief that there is a one-size-fits-all approach to masculinity or femininity and allow individuals to craft a gender performance that suits them first and then can be negotiated as a part of partnership building. Embracing the strength of Caribbean Black women can take some of the pressure off Black men (Chevannes, *Learning to Be a Man* 222–4, Thomas, *Exceptional Violence* 84). It is a fact that Black men are treated unfairly by a racial/capitalist system and for a long time Black women have pulled their own weight to ensure that Black men were not overwhelmed. The desire of our men to be individualistic patriarchs makes them hate women even when those women try to uplift them. As Maude explained in Chapter 2, men want a strong woman to help and that very strength becomes a source of resentment.

The Black community is only as strong as its weakest couple. The possibility of revolutionary power and drive to shape a Black community, healed from racial trauma and less susceptible to passing on generational patterns and mechanisms that hinder us more than serve us, lies within strong families.

Rethinking Gender Justice and Theory

Somewhere in the reification of Western knowledge as all that is good and true, theory became the purview of white researchers in academia and henchmen in global organizations like the United Nations. While calling for more equal power relations with men and the deconstruction of hegemonies that subjugated some people based on race or geographical location, apostles of feminism simultaneously created a (Western) hegemony singularly representative of all women's liberation struggles – feminism. Knowledge hegemony leaves the CC in the position of 'receiver' of knowledge while the West produces. (Western) Theories like feminism become those used in the CC, whether they fit or not. Even when women in the Caribbean try to adjust them, their contributions remain peripheral and marginalized.[4] Feminism is for white women and its base is white supremacy (Hamad 166–75; Jackson 43–61; Zakaria 138). Being a well-balanced Black woman requires an investigation of self. Butch heterosexuality is not about claiming toxic masculine traits like an unwillingness to care for the well-being of others or personal ability to get in touch with emotions. A person cannot and should not be more to anyone than they can be to themselves. Butch heterosexuality is taking up the space necessary in the world to be a fully embodied, comfortable human beyond any kind of binary definition of what that means or looks like. My experience of feminism has led me to conclude that it is not suitable to me and my negotiation of womanhood. Feminism demands "…a form of cultural imperialism that ignores the specificities of different sexual cultures" (Halberstam 122). There are complexities of butchness that feminism omits because they challenge hegemonic formulations of womanhood.

The heavy respectability policing of feminists in the Caribbean has obscured the place of butchness within the movement – whether that butchness is sexually queer or straight. Queer women are accepted into CC feminism if their queerness is not too detectable. In other words even if they were gay they should still strive for 'womanly' characteristics. It helps if they maintain 'femininity' or are femme or keep their relationships contained by a heterosexual marriage. Women labelled 'assertive', 'aggressive' or 'strident' are viewed as out of place as much as they are in men's perspective. While like other theoretical portals womanism is not perfect, the ideology provides belonging and an impetus for theorizing in the present. Alice Walker popularized the term womanist/womanism. In her requiem 'Womanist', Walker invokes the characterization of womanish in her explanation of womanism (19). I concur with the idea that womanism is a full embodiment. It is for loud and bold, conforming and non-conforming people. Some are masculine, others are feminine and still others vacillate without a marked place on the colonial gender spectrum. Womanism is to feminism what purple is to lavender – a completely different shade. One significantly different and needing its own name and meeting its own function. The separation is important and nuanced and without which it would be easy to miss critical philosophical and ideological differences. Unlike feminism, womanism does not embrace hierarchies (whether class or race), patriarchy, heteronormativity or colonial logics. It does not police bodies for respectability or passing. Womanism is inextricable from Blackness and the experience of this socio/racial experience of Caribbean womanhood characterized by constitutive negation and a lack of protection. Those circumstances resulted in a set of mechanisms that Black women used to navigate womanhood in the context of brutal violence. These are racial/ethnic considerations which have formed philosophies of womanhood that have embedded themselves in womanism.

Womanism is not an academic theoretical construct. It belongs to CC women 'in the road'. It is simple language they can use to systematize their experiences – it is poetry and newspaper articles and private diaries. The burden of interpreting those with care and honour rests with trained individuals who may want to use them and not with the owners who should only be responsible for ensuring their voices are heard. Men can be womanist – especially Black men who understand the harm colonialism caused/s Black women. Men who accept their responsibility to decolonize their interactions with the women in their lives – their sisters, aunts, lovers and daughters and who recognize the personal benefits of doing their work are the recruits most desirable. There will be no success fighting historical fractures between Black men and Black women in the CC if Black men continue to cry out for their racial liberation while subjugating Black women along gendered difference. My series colleague, Anne Mauro, writes cogently of the power in re-existing as a stage beyond resistance (66). Resistance can be patriarchally and hierarchically framed but re-existing calls for an honest critique of individualist patriarchy and the harm of it.

My inclusion of men in womanism is not on the same terms as Clenora Hudson-Weems (5). Where Hudson-Weems seems to give Black men a complete pass I invest in believing they can take accountability and be something different. Trauma-informed partnerships demand safe space and asking a man to provide that is not diminishing him as a man or setting him up as an enemy. Black men could function as individualist patriarchs without money, because individualist patriarchy was built on veneer more than reality. Giving Black men a free pass does not make them stronger. This book establishes plantation patriarchy and its symbiotic interrelatedness with PPC. Hudson-Weems attempts to dismiss patriarchy in Africa as immaterial (Hudson-Weems 62–3). However, researchers interested in gender relations in Africa assert that Africa was not free of patriarchy before colonization (Adojoh-Davoh 117; Flynn Bruey 2).

Hudson-Weems concludes that the patriarchy seen in Africa is connected to organized religion including Muslim and Christianity (62–3). It is the connection between religion and female subjugation that I have a discomfort with an embrace of religion in the womanist framework. I do not include religion in my reworking although worship of trees and other miracles of nature is useful.

(White) God the father, the son and them moving on the wind over and above everything is the triumvirate at the base of female subjugation. Decolonizing relations between Black men and women and making room for butch heterosexual approaches to womanhood are incompatible with any religion that upholds female subjugation and colonial logics. It is pointless to want liberation as a woman and want a white god too. While I have time for some of the positions put forward by Courtney Bryant in *Erotic Defiance* that advocate for a different way to see Black women and their sexuality, her adherence to Christian principles and Christian gives rise to a paradox in her argument. These kinds of paradoxes result in religious fundamentalism which is harmful and hurtful. It takes substantial amounts of energy, results in cognitive dissonance and intellectual dishonesty to exist in a mindset of wanting Black liberation and a white god. For instance, Bryant decries the damage that Western culture has done to the self and sexual image of Black women while at the same time invoking Jesus Christ, a Western-made construct throughout her writing (Bryant xv–xvi). Whatever the question is in Barbados and the CC, the wrong answer is white Western religion. Religion has been used to decry the familial and sexual expression of working-class Caribbeans. It has been used to vilify and harass other gender expressions and queerness and it has been used to uphold and legitimate patriarchal and colonial logics (hooks, *The Will to Change* 18; Hall, *Civilising Subjects* 300; Johnson 53; Sheller 46). While I understand that there is a religious movement that provided a strong impetus for resistance struggle in the CC, even the indigenous religion, Rastafari, has been a stifling ordeal for women[5] (Dunkley 3). Certainly, even if femme (queer and het) women have eked out religious accommodation over time, Butch women still struggle with acceptance. Religion, like the judiciary, is a social whip used to stoutly defend male domination, PPC and adherence to status quo. Caribbean women have never had a seamless or uncomplicated relationship with feminism. A move away from feminism to womanism allows a woman to become firmly balanced in herself. It is another step in a positive direction but until the distance between theory and lived experience is closed by embedding autonomy within the state, there will be issues of constitutive negation to contend with.

Rethinking the State – Nationalism Reclaimed

An entire analysis of the Caribbean state is beyond the scope of this section but what I do propose to do is focus on women's organizing, the judicature and the formation of nationalism to contemplate what a different relationship between the state and its citizen and citizens at the family level could be. One of the significant failings of the feminist movement in the Caribbean was that many representatives and proponents lived what I call 'the hypocrisy of plantation'. While they agitated for policies and changes that seemed geared to women, they also presided over a portrayal of, especially domestic violence that made it the problem of working-class and poor women. While middle- and upper-class women saw themselves as the face and intellectual ferment of the women's movement, they were wives to husbands, sisters to brothers, mothers to sons who carried on clandestine extramarital affairs, were emotionally and even other kinds of abusive and were perpetrators of sexual harassment and abuse in the wider society. bell hooks explains the phenomenon well and how it leads to bitterness. She explains that, "all over the world women live with men in states of lovelessness. They live and they mourn" (*The Will to Change* 14).

The bitterness can seep into relations with other women and affect women's organizing – such is the long reach of patriarchal degradation. The result is that the women's liberation movement is splintered and riddled with contradictions that allow traditional gender norms to continue basically unchallenged in Barbados. There is no public position that can be taken separately and removed from a personal decision. Additionally, the class element of women's organizing meant that the womanhood conceived was Victorian/bourgeoisie. Women were to be feminine, in their place, in the service of their men folk and boxed in by binary relations to masculinity and manhood. Women themselves became gatekeepers of other women who were seen to step beyond the prescribed parameters. In exchange for being 'good women', they get married and are respectable. bell hooks explains that even within single-parent homes women can and do invest in patriarchy (*The Will to Change* 24).

Mauro offers a list that practitioners providing services to the Black community could use to make their services safer and trauma-informed. I think her call to action is a good guide that the CC women's movement should consider in reshaping the sector. She encourages practitioners to be self-reflective. She proposes, inter alia, 'healing the personal self' as a central part of decolonizing work and offering help to others (67). The current CC feminist movement has skeletons of colonialism, white supremacy and Victorian respectability buried within it that are harmful to the very women the movement purports to assist. The aim of fighting for women's agency in the Caribbean is not to create a hegemonic feminist enterprise. It is not for middle- and upper-class women to know better than other women what they need. It is also not to prescribe a particular type of femininity or performance of femininity that is seen as 'good' and others that are seen as harsh or too masculine. The CC women's movement is to create grassroots, inclusive women's liberation where the goals are set by the masses and the funding is derived from the CC so that there is internal control over the agenda and longevity of programming. It should be organized beyond narrow party politics, and individuals who are politically exposed should have to declare that. As is the habit in broader political organizing, the salt of the earth Caribbean people cannot be seen as an inconvenient mass which can be activated or dismissed as it suits an agenda or career. Caribbean women must be seen as the owners of their own liberation and included in its making at every point.

This point is not only related to women's organizing but the broader CC nationalist and political movement. After passing the Public Order Act of 1970, which stymied growing discontent about continued PPC and rising Black consciousness in the Barbadian masses, Errol Barrow expected the Barbadian public to support an agenda of change that he thought was measured and appropriate (Watson 49–53). Charismatic leadership is a leadership of trickery. It is a leadership of political gaslighting and manipulating for the benefit of the politourgeoise. What should be matters of principle become political hoops to be scored. The politourgeoise have replaced the white bourgeoisie in contemporary Barbados. They have continued to be purveyors of a neoliberal agenda that creates displaced citizens – women (especially those who operate outside traditional rigid gender rules), queer folk, disabled, mad and the poor. These categories are what I term citizenless citizens. Citizenless citizens are those that capitalism deems useless or burdensome and for whom "...the promises of citizenship have long been bankrupt, and their ability to participate (in markets, in political life) has long been circumscribed" (Thomas, *Exceptional Violence* 42). The national imagination in Barbados and the CC is ruptured. Everyone is confused as to why youth are opting to live and exist within a life of crime that threatens the overall well-being of their societies. Human nature is to exert energy in the things that have a tangible personal value and benefit. There are many people in the Caribbean that nationalism no longer is of interest to, because it does not change their material circumstances. Whether the women of Barbados vote in general elections or not, they are no better now to secure maintenance with respect to their children.

The Black men in the CC may be more willing to release their stranglehold on the control of women and children if they have a greater stake in the business and political life of Barbados. For Barbados and the CC to become the kind of society that stops doing harm to its own citizens through upholding archaic and harmful colonial relics it must be brutally honest about the changes and their solutions. There must be space for "mourning, adaptation, and forgiveness" (Thomas, *Exceptional Violence* 110). This is not work with a finite beginning and end, but it is liberation in action – "reinhabiting the world, a process that is necessarily ongoing" (Thomas, *Exceptional Violence* 110). Recitizening people deprived of full social inclusion cannot be a top-down approach. There are numerous anecdotes of how politics has failed the Caribbean region – many researched and documented. Jamaica is known for the nexus between politics and organized crime, but the book *Caribbean Charisma* reveals this pattern is Caribbean-wide, and most territories are more similar than different. None is more revered than Owen Seymour Arthur as a charismatic Caribbean leader. I bought my first house at the age of eighteen and escaped a vicious cycle of family abuse under his vision and stewardship.

At the same time, if I apply a two-handed approach to his tenure in office, I must admit that he was the purveyor of the 'politics of inclusion' which has led Barbados more towards the neoliberal agenda where the almighty dollar is King – a soulless capitalist society where not life, nor heritage, nor anything is sacred.[6] The politics of inclusion was Owen Arthur's response to the economic crisis of the early 1990s. To bolster Barbados in preparation to go to the International Monetary Fund (IMF), Arthur created a 'buy in' strategy across Barbados. Arthur, who had studied and worked in the early years of his career in Jamaica clearly knew the perils of structural adjustment and the harsh IMF economic policies that could destabilize a Caribbean territory. Arthur's strategy was to bring together stakeholders from across the various sectors of Barbados – civil society, the churches, corporate sector and unaligned community influencers. Out of the effort the world-famous social partnership model was formed and Barbados' crisis staved off for a few years. The less discussed but drastically impactful side effect of the politics of inclusion is that charismatic leadership and the all-powerful political party ethos were further embedded in Barbados. Dissent was abhorred as something that was slowing down Barbados' ability to be ready and fight off the financial crisis. Long after the crisis, the tenants of the politics of inclusion remain. Political and social justice actors are driven by wanting recognition of their power of influence. That power leads to them being courted and subsumed into governmental structures and the party and its ever-important patronage (Thomas, *Exceptional Violence* 50). This has made everything in Barbados political and blurred important lines of the separation of powers. It has in effect rendered Barbados' democracy dysfunctional. So how does a dysfunctional state foster functional family life? Short answer is, it cannot. The society itself must stop being abusive. A part of that is giving voice to the fact that Barbados is a contemporary plantation where the product of capitalism may no longer be sugar or bananas but the logics that abuse and subjugate Black people, Black women and citizenless citizens (e.g. the mad, indigent) remain (DeGruy 100, Thomas, *Exceptional Violence* 79). Men and women take a battering living in plantation societies where anti-blackness is baked into every system and nowhere is that played out like in the judicial system.

Another system in the Caribbean in significant need of repair, decolonization and restoration is the judiciary. Even members of the politourgeoise, like Errol Barrow had reason to complain about the level of non-functionality of what is to be the Caribbean justice system (Watson 41). Justice and the juridical procedure in Barbados and the CC were never connected because a plantation is an unjust mechanism. Particularly in family matters, the courts in the Caribbean are unsafe spaces underpinned by logics of punishment, Black womanhood as immoral and to be harnessed and racial and classist notions of dysfunctionality synonymous with Blackness. The family court is an arena where the unresolved gender tensions in the Caribbean play out daily. As Suzanne LaFont explains:

> Historical, cultural and economic features of [Caribbean] society have led to a tradition of female independence which is in many ways contrary to the dominant ideology of male hegemony. This generates conflict between the sexes[SIC] as men and women vie for power within their relationships. … The Family Courts as an arena for gender relations and the Family Laws as examples of how the dominant ideology is imposed on the lower classes (LaFont 4–5).

It is not a class-specific experience as much as it is a gendered one. The judiciary in Barbados is used as a central tool in the arsenal of upholding individualistic patriarchy. The courts have a long history of over policing and punishing womanhood (Green 144). The juridical system in Barbados keeps the class stratification of plantation intact. The magistrate's courts hear family cases and matters where the couple are in cohabiting and visiting relations while married couples' matters are heard in high court. Different statutes also govern people based on whether parties are married, visiting or cohabiting. The magistrate's court is not a court of record. In other words, most of the judgements and decisions made in that court are not written. Further, there is no research department associated with the court. These two factors are significant examples of the structural issues associated with family matters in the magistracy. Many women are at a disadvantage because they often cannot get transcripts or information about their cases. For instance, a woman fleeing Barbados from the Caribbean will struggle to provide overseas authorities with official documents although they may have active cases before the courts. Another major unresolved issue that affects women's safety in family court is the difference between the letter of law and its operation, as Edith Clarke highlights. Clarke uses the perennial issue of child maintenance and the low compliance of CC Black men to support their children financially to show how women are frustrated by the judiciary (and the police) (Clarke 76–80).

I use the more contemporary Barbadian example of CAP 130A, the Domestic Violence Protection Order Act. In 2023, the Caribbean Court of Justice (CCJ) handed down a decision in OO v BK and Another. The case, familiarly known as the 'former spouse' case, is one that challenged some of the Victorian remnants of class vestiges in relation to family structures in the Caribbean and which affects the granting of Protection Orders. Barbados' first passing of the Domestic Violence Protection Orders Act in 1992 did not make provisions for women living in visiting or cohabiting relations to be protected. As Mary Spooner notes Protection Orders in the Caribbean were more geared towards reconciliation than ensuring the safety and separation of the situation (Spooner 118) (130 A (1993) 7(1)C). The Act was also heteronormative in that it conceived partners to a marriage as only husband and wife. Census and research data point to the fact that visiting or cohabiting relationships are still major familial formations in Barbados. Therefore, there was a significant part of the population that the 1992 Act did not cover, and this was a part of the push by women's advocates to have the legislation expanded. The 2016 amended CAP 130A is a well-drafted, modern piece of legislation. The United Nations funded amendments included training for judicial officers in the use of CAP 130A as well as the need for it. However, the amended CAP 130A runs counter to individualistic patriarchy and the rules of PPC. The Act is seen as destroying families and being a part of draconian foreign policies to oppress Caribbean men (Spooner 118). Although the Law was as close to a perfect statute as the women's advocates who fought for its revision could have hoped, the Act is thwarted and misinterpreted in courts to the disadvantage of women daily as the ruling of the CCJ elucidates.

One of the facts that gave rise to the former spouse appeal is that the judiciary of Barbados was narrowly interpreting former spouse as related to individuals in a legal marriage only, despite the 2016 amendment explanatory notes made clear that the intention was to expand the categories of relationships covered for victims of violence to seek protection. The CCJ ruling makes it clear that the interpretation of former spouse should be expansive enough to cover people in cohabitational and visiting relationships (37 c, d, e, f). The constitutive negation that is a historical reality of women's lives is highlighted as a continuing in the CCJ judgement:

> The appellant, appeared before the Magistrate, urgently seeking the court's protection, **the Magistrate was sufficiently impressed that there was violence or the threat of violence because the Magistrate made a protection order in relation to her child**. The Magistrate, however, declined to make one in favour of the appellant with whom the child lived. The Magistrate seemed to be more concerned with interrogating the nature of her current relationship with her ex than with her safety or with the aggressive conduct of her former partner towards her. Instead of paying attention to the violent inclination of the man, the Magistrate chose to school the woman on jurisdictional aspects of the law. The Magistrate asked her a series of questions regarding her opinion of how the law applied to her circumstances. The Magistrate then concluded that, because of the answers she gave, the court lacked jurisdiction and she did not qualify for a protection order for herself. (70 c, d, e, f)

The patriarchy that women in the CC are fighting is not only against male brutality in the home. Male abusive behaviour in the Caribbean is upheld by a well-defined culture that legitimates this behaviour as a god-given right, normal and natural. The court is an instrument of that belief. There are two other significant ways that (usually) women seeking Protection Orders are frustrated. First, they are denied maintenance orders as stipulated under the Act and second, they are forced to co-parent with their perpetrators without state mechanisms of safety. Without a maintenance arrangement for children, many women exist in manufactured poverty – financial abuse used as punishment for them daring to move themselves from abuse. Women are the ones removed from the house, despite the fact that many men move into homes owned by women because children and property are seen as the rights of men. Individualistic patriarchy is, as Deborah Thomas explains, a "boundar[y] that mark[s] the limits of sociocultural citizenship that have been rooted in dominant nationalist notions related to families, economics and politics" (Thomas, *Exceptional Violence* 43).

Conclusion

What I have tried to do in this chapter – perhaps seamlessly, perhaps not – is to contemplate the changes necessary and possible in heterosexual coupling that move Black women and men beyond harmful colonial divisions and patriarchal performances of masculinity AND femininity. To have dominion over women, women must be opposite to men and devoid of their own masculinity. Victorian performances of womanhood are a set of values about womanhood that make it supple for patriarchal manhood. They are a set of values that ran counter to those necessary for Black women to survive the experience of individualistic patriarchy and PPCs which are created through violence, degradation of women, children, the disabled and Black people generally. I outline in this chapter that the liberation of Black heterosexual coupling cannot be rescued in a vacuum. It will be the result of individual work done to redefine and reshape Black femininity and Black masculinity. Moving beyond the self-hate and divisions created between Black men and women requires recognizing the effects of trauma as the result of the Transatlantic kidnapping, forced labour and racialization and that these realities are those undergirding the modern Caribbean project. Butch heterosexuality as a performance of womanhood which reveals the tensions in heterosexual gender relations in the Caribbean acts as a lens through which rigid gender norms can be challenged.

Organic theory making is important to creating the kind of ideology that will be directly applicable to the decolonization left to be done in the Caribbean. While linguists, historians and sociologists, to name a few, have been innovative in developing theories to reflect the historical and social nuances of the Caribbean I think gender theorists have been lazy. They have depended on feminist logics and others external to the CC that have alienated, frustrated and divided women. By proposing womanism and thinking through a reworking here, I am not trying to be pedantic. I am taking up my space in knowledge making and asking my sisters in the Caribbean to be comfortable to do the same – to know that they are invited to do the same and that they are important in that process.

The extent to which heterosexual coupling can change is hemmed in by the society and the extent that a society can function in support of a new place and understanding for women. That requires persuading men that their own liberation is bound up with that of women. The way that people organize their family units is inextricably tied to the kind of state they live in and how that state constructs masculinity and femininity. PPC utilizes the judiciary as one of the major arms that legitimates it. Further, social services and the political functioning of the state create unsafety for Black men and Black women. I am advocating for partnerships where Black men and Black women use a trauma-informed, honest approach to bolster themselves and their unions. To be successful, these unions must be erotic and pleasurable but they must also be formed through difficult conversations about politics and nationalism and the Caribbean liberation movement. For Black men to see themselves in nationalism there must be a place for them in decision making and the corporate life of Barbados. Barbadian men are being marginalized but it is not by their women. It is by the politourgeoise in the country that is taking up too much space with personal agendas and upholding systemic structures left by the white patriarchs who developed PPC instead of dismantling them. It is in their personal reflections, the beginning of different relations with their women that Black men can find a way out of patriarchy and capitalism – both of which have never worked for them. I agree with bell hooks that there is a need to create literature, research and rewards that encourage men to love, to think about love and to seek different ways to love. Many Caribbean women live in fear of men as hooks rightly asserts that love and fear cannot cohabit in the same space (*The Will to Change*, 8–10). hooks and I concur that (Caribbean) men are tired. The high levels of violence among them signals the discontent, hopelessness and despair. This chapter proposes trauma-informed partnerships as a tangible set of values and practices that Black men and women can engage to heal the division between them. Safe space (e.g. safer emotional engagement in partnerships, but also physical spaces like beaches, women's groups and family groups, enforcement of sexual harassment legislation); support (e.g. better access to social services and financial aid); the willingness to grow together and separately, adjusting unequal power relations and reclamation of the Caribbean nationalism/decolonization project in Black partnerships are a few of the critical elements of change.

Notes

1 See Anne Schneider and Helen Ingram's *Policy Design for Democracy*.
2 See Matthew Parker *The Sugar Barons* (Parker 9–11; 116) for an explanation of the significance of the Drax Family in Barbados.
3 The Mia Mottley led administration gave prime crown land in Bridgetown to the private entity, Afreximbank. The fact was revealed in the National Parliamentary Budgetary presentation in March 2025.

4 See the concerns about feminism outlined by DAWN and how they reconceptualized feminism to better suit the Caribbean. Their idea of intersectional analysis of women's lives and women's empowerment was popularized but never connected to the Global South women who were integral to outline these approaches (Sen 18–20, Zakaria 58–61).

5 See also the memoir of Safiya Sinclair *How to Say Babylon*.

6 As I write this section on 26 March 2025, a thirteen-year-old, beautiful Black boy, named Shawnaton lost his life to unfettered gun crime while the politourgeoise that comprise our current government worry about their position before the camera and the public media optics. Walk good Shawnaton. The ancestors who know and understand violence well will comfort you.

4 Redefining Heterosexual Partnership

Building Anti-Patriarchal Relationships by Prioritizing Healing

The contemporary Commonwealth Caribbean (CC) is considered a zone of periphery – one characterized by complex social problems. At the same time it continues to be portrayed as an oasis of gentle fresh breeze and pristine vistas – a land of potential if only it could be rid of its dysfunctional Black population. That frontier view, necessary in legitimating CC exploitation is a veneer that masks the ravages of plantation – an ahistoric one that CC intellectuals have vehemently fought (Gregg 32–5). The CC was at the centre of modernity. Contact between Europe and Africa in the CC gave rise to the logics that underpin racial capitalism, heteronormative gender relations and the masculinities and femininities that normalize patriarchy. Gender relations in the CC are no more replicas of Victorian values than they are direct retentions from African substrate cultures. Rather, the Caribbean had a set of sex and gender relations that gave rise to the embrace of Victorian values.

Anyone, including theorists, researchers and social justice advocates who omit the Caribbean will only ever be arriving at a partial answer in the explanation of modernity (Thomas, *Exceptional Violence* 93). I say that as much for foreigners as I say it for those of us working within the Caribbean intellectual tradition and the (Diasporic) Black radical tradition that is its progeny. Depend on feminist or Victorian models of womanhood cannot assist us in knowing ourselves as Black women because our experiences of womanhood significantly shaped both of those enterprises. I agree with AnaLouise Keating that feminist theorizing is stuck, "circling around a few contentious issues, locked into several ruts, trapped by…oppositional thinking" (32–3). Nowhere can the hostile separatist results of feminist-based gender theorizing be seen more than in CC conversations about gender. I hope that the reconfigurations of womanhood offered here can eventually offer Black men and Black women alternative talking points and approaches. Making intimate relations healthier and different ways is the ground zero of Black revolution.

The truth is, the most honest summation of intimate relationships in the Caribbean is that men are hurting and women are hurting. Descendants of Africans kidnapped and forced into the slavery enterprise in this region of the world have been left to process the brutality without adequate access to

DOI: 10.4324/9781003518709-5

mass therapy and support. Although it has been established in many ways, including through the music of Bob Marley and Tarus Riley, that the plantation is not just physical space but a way of thinking and being, enough has not done to stop the ratoons of the system that stubbornly show up in the treatment of women and girls; the disparate levels of childhood sexual abuse across the region and high levels of self-deprecation causing our lack of national empathy. In his seminal work on the development of creole societies, Kamau Brathwaite writes that, "creole society was stable because the unprivileged and underprivileged within it conform to the system, its divisions, and its restrictions. The whole slave system began as a coercive one, but developed into a system of consent" (Brathwaite 193). Wrestling freedom from rigid hierarchical structures demands a rejection of plantation norms.

By starting this work with invoking our ancestors, I am not trying to overstate the amount of power enslaved African women had to determine their destiny and sexual relations. I think the caution that Halberstam calls for in transposing our understanding of gender relations and performances today to other historical times is important (45–8). What I am trying to show with the ratooning model of gender performance in Barbados and the CC is that Black women faced hideous atrocities and the womanhood they developed – that they needed to have – was affected by their social environment. CC women's refusal to be hurt and subjugated by patriarchal adherence did not arise with any Western feminist agenda. They arose out of the defiance, resilience and experience of generations of our Black ancestors who refused to break or in some cases die under the horror of plantation and colonialism. I am also not making a case for butch heterosexuality to only be seen as refusal. As Halberstam reminds us:

> Female masculinity is a particularly fruitful site of investigation because it has been vilified by heterosexist and feminist/womanist programs alike; unlike male femininity, which fulfills a kind of ritual function in male homosocial cultures, female masculinity is generally received by hetero- and homo-normative cultures as a pathological sign of misidentification and maladjustment, as longing to be and to have power that is always just out of reach (9).

I believe that female masculinity has the power to disrupt the heteropatriarchal gender binary the most. While heterosexual men can choose to ignore or be ambivalent about queer gender identities, confronting men with the reality that not every heterosexual woman is a feminine woman changes heterosexual norms and expectations. I believe it is the major reasons that masculine women in the Caribbean are treated with such contempt. Female masculinity complicates 'straightness', and women seen as out of place – including strong Black independent women – become explainable in historical ways. I believe that while Halberstam's work on female masculinity is a seminal and critical intervention, he falls into some of the very traps in his discussion of female masculinity as he advocates for fixing. I believe that there are examples through the book where he conflates gender identity with sexual orientation and butchness with transness (15; 20–21; 27). By examining female masculinity in the heterosexual orientation, I hope I have unlocked alternative calibrations of female masculinity.

In encouraging historians to move beyond political, economic and social categories of interpreting archives of Transatlantic slavery, Tim Downs extolls the value of applying Black feminist theoretical frameworks (193). While I agree with expanding the analysis beyond these categories or at least to put these in conversations with other areas like gender, citizenship from below and Afrofuturism (as I have tried to do with this work), feminism is not the understanding of self in which Black women will find answers about the next move in our liberation. For one, feminism in the Caribbean has upheld patriarchy bound up in respectability and the classist Victorian ideal of womanhood. Heterosexual gender performances and relations need to be widened and deepened beyond predominantly white stereotypes that have never represented Black women fully and which Black women – Sojourner Truth[1] (one of the most known) in her *Ain't I A Woman* speech – have refuted for centuries. While I do recognize the value of contributions labelled Black feminism, I have no investment in legitimating feminism.

I believe that in trying to fit ourselves under the feminist umbrella, Black women, breathed life into what is otherwise a useless framework at the expense of building womanism as our own theorem. I hope that this book can be helpful to Caribbean women who have long (and rightfully) had fraught relationship with feminism. Feminism has done harm to Black women and it has done damage to women whose femininity is not white or normative. By reformulating femininity in expansive ways, Black presentations of femininity hopefully find more credence and legitimacy. Calling oneself womanist signals a praxis. While I am writing this book I am also working with partners to secure funding and to deliver programming to Black men and boys that introduce them to some of the information about gender I am thinking through here. Change has never and will never be generated by writing alone. Along with writing, the audacity to test our interventions in the petri dish of life is paramount. Intimate relations must be ordered differently, speak to and raise our sons differently and call our male work colleagues to different order. I choose womanism not because it is a perfect theoretical space but exactly because feminism isn't either as much investment and time has been given to it as Black intellectuals. I also believe that assigning 'protofeminism' to any women's resistance (such as Truth) is appropriation. I think it is better to leave these women's contributions categorized as a rich archive of women's resistance to oppression. Some of that oppression was fought using the white-supremacist and exclusionary framework that is feminism, and others have organized under other formations more spacious and decolonial, such as womanism. Alice Walker said that womanism was to feminism what purple was to lavender; I say that women's resistance is the progenitor, and feminism and womanism equal daughters of a multi-sibling family.

Further, as I document in this book, the CC has a historical experience of its own that gave rise to performances of womanhood which made sense given the high levels of exploitation, sexual and other types of brutality women faced. Thomas Thistlewood's diaries show stratification between classes of white men in the CC. What kept them together was brutality and greed. To achieve that they were allegiant to whiteness and some level of fraternity was required but that fraternity was governed by their egos and unfettered control of their individual turfs. The fraternity also becomes complicated by race in that Black men were allowed into patriarchy but on a differentiated scale. The patriarchal formation which started as the purview of white men was embraced by Black men and embedded in the nationalist political movement. Can Black men be patriarchs? Yes they can. It is not about showing the preservation of a patriarchy they were cut off from in Africa. It is the fact that patriarchy is a colonial logic that legitimated Black death in the Atlantic world. Black men instead of deconstructing individualistic patriarchy have embraced and reified it. Plantations were sites of contradiction, excess, exploitation and venereal disease. The historical legacies of PPC and individualistic patriarchy have caused harm to gender relations between men and women. Caribbean women's performances of a femininity that kept individualist patriarchy in check were present from the earliest days of plantation and they ratooned through to what I label butch heterosexuality.

Perhaps the fact that I have the comfort and audacity to want to be identified for my butchness when I can pass for my heterosexuality is testament to how far the fight for women's equality has come. However, that I have wonderful relationships with Black men as friends and toxic and tumultuous relationships with them as lovers is a signpost for how far there still is to go. I have also thought a lot about womanhood in Barbados and how it is understood systemically. I have worked as an advocate in Barbados providing services to women and girls affected by gender-based violence including sexual violence for two decades. As I saw the various challenges of women, I recognized that as much as this is a fight for our individual liberation – it is also as much a fight for decolonization of gender norms and systemic changes. Women's organizing in Barbados, like the wider nationalist political movement, has stopped short of uprooting the firmly entrenched colonial logics. There is no commitment to ensuring that the masses of Caribbean women see themselves represented in the methods and themes of the movement. The overall weak historical record about what has been achieved by women social justice warriors is perhaps an unrelated problem but equally limiting to our work (Gregg xix).

I first got the ideas for this book from interactions with colleagues around conference and social spaces.[2] The state of the relationship between

Black women and Black men is another reason I wanted to take the time to think though the ideas I presented here. It feels to me as though Black women and men live in deep suspicion and loathing of each other. Creating stronger partnerships in the Black community requires conversations that change our outlook and ideas of each other. I am reclaiming masculinity for all my foremothers who were punished and criminalized for being "manly, aggressive and vulgar" (Gregg 37). Even as I honour their strength, I hope to make their historical legacy more attractive as an option for negotiating life for Black girls AND a viable option for partnership for Black boys. A strong Black woman does not emasculate a Black man – she is a part of his healing and restoration. I am not suggesting that every Black girl or woman has to identify herself as Butch heterosexual. What I am suggesting is that Black femininity has always been an expansive receptacle where the girlies of us exist and the not so girly of us exist. Resistance to upholding a femininity that is only needed by patriarchs and patriarchy gives more opportunity to explore each other and support each other in our collective experience on 'womanness'. This thought occurred to me when I kept embarrassingly referring to an agendered colleague as 'girl' during out chit chat. I felt poorly for my constant slip and in reflecting on why it happened I realized the elasticity that has always been present in Caribbean womanhoods. 'Girl' is an affectionate expression used among Black woman, woman-identifying and woman presenting friends as they talk in Black Diasporic communities including the CC (where I was born and raised) and America (which has a large Caribbean descended and African Diaspora). The important part of my reflection about my slip is not that I was seeing my colleague as female – the important part of the explanation was that their presentation as a Black agender person was familiar and included in a womahoood expansive enough for all of us. 'Girl' as a greeting in the Black community can be as agendered or queer and/or as Butch as all of us.

Black women have spent a lot of time trying to explain what we are not, wholly less time was devoted to defining what we are. For instance, despite our refutations of the 'angry black woman' trope, it remains pervasive and it is assigned to as part of a strategy of dismissal. Black men, especially those invested in upholding and maintaining patriarchy, white women invested in white supremacy and even other Black women who have not taken the time to reflect on their inbuilt self-hatred and/or generational patterns of abuse are some of the categories of people keeping this view of Black women vogue. In this book, I claimed the angry Black woman as a resilient, defiant, smartass, who adapted to plantation and survived for her adaptation. My attempt was not to describe Black womanhood overall but a particular type of femininity – only one of many – completely uninvested in upholding patriarchy or any other social system but the right to be and to be respected for being. In extolling the legitimacy of Butch heterosexuality, I am not glorifying the practice of toxic masculinity. I am hopefully creating room for masculinity to be broadened and to benefit from existing simultaneously with femininity. Perhaps it is through Butch heterosexual mothers that Black boys learn that crying and good welding skills can exist in the same personage without the one eviscerating the other.

Butchness does not preclude us as Black women from needing therapy and trauma-informed mental health services – the Black race needs to collectively heal. All of us have a part in that. The healing is not from female masculinity AKA 'anger'. The healing is from the damage of subjugation manifested as high levels of sexual abuse of the girl child; intimate partner violence that disproportionately affects woman and a state machinery that holds us in constitutive negation. This book focuses on both self-identification and social negotiation of femininity. Our liberation is to be found in cacophonous discourse and not in a waylaid and quiet movement that only deals with individual women and not the systemic strangulation of Black womanhood embedded in the plantation. I advocate for heterosexual relations becoming trauma-informed spaces of mutual effort, safety and growth. I also hope to encourage a deeper and more genuine attempt by us as Black Caribbean women to be more understanding and tolerant of each other and to stop our policing of each other on behalf of individualistic patriarchy and plantation patriarchal culture.

In retrospect, I learned a lot about living in a 'female' body from my grandmother. I never saw her depend on a man financially. I also saw her choose clothing that allowed her to be able to ply her trades – digging potatoes and yams, herding animals and butchering them. She was a strong woman and she cared for us but her affection was in her cooking and washing – not kisses or hugs. Were she a man, that would have been seen as optimal care and anyone complaining about the missing hugs and kisses would have been absurd; the totem pole demands difference of performance of womaness and manness. I was not deprived of hugs and kisses as a child – I never liked them. Not all of us thrive on having our bodies touched and personal space invaded. My granny's kind of care was more comfortable and appreciated by me. Frank honesty as CC people unearths that, rigid gender norms and heteropatriarchal constructs have always been outside of our lived experience as a people. It is not historically accurate to say, that agenderism or butchness are Western imports because these approaches to womanhood represent the way I saw personhood acted by my grandmother or (m)any of the women I met when I couriered her pork or pudding and souse to sell. I am not suggesting that the women I met as a girl were agender – that would be presumptive and perhaps also historically inaccurate. What I mean is that Black womanhood was never monolithic and unlike white womanhood which was marketed as coherent, exclusive and intolerant of femininities that were not mainstream, Black womanhood has always held space for multiple performances of womanhood.

It is only as an adult that I would learn my grandmother was a survivor of intimate partner violence. She had left the alcoholism and constant beatings of my grandfather and returned to her maternal family plot. What I contend in this book is that Black women's interactions with dehumanization as a feature of metamorphizing Africans into Black/slaves and the resulting high levels of violence against women – both structural and individual – have shaped how Black women perform femininity. The brutality continued through the post-independence years and into the contemporary moment. Some CC Black women have developed a specific kind of femininity – a female masculinity – that I believe fits within the identity 'butch'. Butch is a marker of gender and not sexuality. In my own experience of my grandmother and my own understanding of myself as a woman, it was possible to be a woman who slept with men but also embrace different negotiations of our relation with men than the traditional ideation that underpins the term 'heterosexual'.

What I have done in this work hopefully adds "categories of possibility for [Caribbean] women" *beyond* the social order that still binds us to plantation (Gregg 35–6). I hope I have added to the conceptual repertoire of Caribbean womanhood in away exemplary of Linden Lewis' assertion that Caribbean people must be engaged in a constant "reclaiming, adjusting and reconstructing [of] social relations, particularly gendered relations…" (2) I tried to connect contemporary embodiments of Black femininity with their historical, social and political contexts. I conceive gender and womanhood as interdisciplinary and transdisciplinary – to understand them requires willingness to travel through history, Caribbean studies, anti-oppressive frameworks like critical studies, (Black) sociology and womanist studies. I am mindful of the pigeon holing of works such as this as gender or (Black) woman's studies because I concur with Judith Butler that, "the complexity of gender requires an interdisciplinary and postdisciplinary set of discourses in order to resist the domestication of gender studies or women studies within the academy and to radicalize the notion of [womanist][3] critique" (xxxiv). My disciplinary unruliness purposely centres this book in womanism rather than feminism as an action that calls out the whiteness, dangers and gaps of that philosophy to attention.[4]

I hope that this book can help in a few ways to kindle necessary conversations with Caribbean women, men and between men and women. Heterosexual CC men need new frameworks to think about and view their lovers. Black CC men have bought into the toxicity and patriarchy that were pervasive features of building plantation societies. I hope that this book can help Caribbean men to understand that Caribbean women are strong but that strength should be read as agency, resistance and survival strategy rather than as confrontational, challenge or emasculation. I also hope that discussing masculinity as something that women possess and perform and not just as the domain of men, changes the discussion and perception about women who do not perform femininity in 'traditional' ways. Much of the way that femininity is constructed in the Caribbean has been given to us by Western notions of what it means to be a 'good' woman. In other words, it is a colonial relic to understand CC Black female gender performance through the template set down for white Victorian women who were operating in patriarchal families (Moore 96–7). The result has been pathologization of many features of Black femininity that do not fit the Victorian mould seamlessly.

I hope this book has answered three questions for readers: (1) how does societal experience influence and shape the social construction of gender, (2) What am I reading as a plantation society in contemporary terms and (3) Why have I chosen the word 'butch' for the performance of womanhood I try to frame? Gender is a set of societal roles and expectation assigned to bodies based largely on the genitalia perceived at birth. Gender is inherently simplified because it is only meant to apply to (white)[5] bodies that are unambiguous and polar. Gender is built on a differential basis – what is man and masculine oppositely corresponds to what is woman and feminine and vice versa. Gender then is at the heart of patriarchal worldviews because it enables a power disparity in favour of men and maleness. For that differential to be held rigidly in place, women must be outside of masculinity which is the major ingredient for the making of man and maleness. The construction of gender as polar positions of difference creates erasures for bodies that do not operate in unambiguous or polar ways and it also causes involuntary conflations for those that do.

In this book, I suggested that the creation of PPC and plantation depends on the conflations arising out of the social construction of gender. Judith Butler argues that a major element of the social construction of gender is what she terms 'compulsory heterosexuality' (xxx). Compulsory sexuality inter alia, makes it possible for "naturalization of both heterosexuality and masculine sexual agency [as] discursive constructions nowhere accounted for but everywhere assumed…" (Butler 58). As much as research and activism in sexuality and queer studies have legitimated different gender and sexual identities, women who sleep with men are still assigned automatic gender roles and foredetermined investment in compulsory heterosexuality. Here I am reading heterosexuality not just as a sexual act but also acceptance of the patriarchal plantation culture that is pervasive in Barbados and the CC. Once a woman has sexual relationships with men, there is only one set of gender norms that she is automatically assigned. These include specific performances of femininity that present her as submissive, subordinated and participatory in a detrimental system without agency just by virtue of her being a woman in (sexual) relation with men. It is my contention that the social construction of gender propagated by patriarchy has never been the reality of CC Black women, and the disparity between the truth of women's experiences and the fiction of Black men, is the real cause of gender friction.

It is important to consider the intersection between gender and other identities to correctly analyse the experience of womanhood in the CC. Butler explains in *Gender Trouble*:

> If one "is" a woman, that is surely not all one is; the term fails to be exhaustive, not because a pregendered "person" transcends the specific paraphernalia of its gender, but because gender is not always constituted coherently or consistently in different historical contexts and because gender intersects with racial, class, ethnic, sexual and regional modalities of discursively constituted identities. As a result, it becomes impossible to separate out "gender" from the political and cultural intersections in which it is invariably produced and maintained (4).

Gender is a foundational oppressive mechanism in the construction of a plantocratic patriarchal society. Chapter 1 revealed that massa was as much massa because he had control over land and financial resources as he was because he had access to women's bodies. The case of Thomas Thistlewood reveals that his idea of being a free man had as much to do with his holdings as with his liberal access to the bodies of his 'slave' possessions. So significant a symbol of individualistic patriarchy is having access to the emotional, physical and sexual labour of multiple women, that it created a new kind of social status marker across the CC that remains with the largely male politourgeoise guarding their access to women's bodies as a continued privilege marker (Moore 113; 117). Thus, a massa was not only white as time progressed in the CC. Black men who had access to privilege through jobs which enabled them to have multiple relationships with women, usually for the financial gain of economically struggling women, got a pass to the club of massa/patriarch.

Black motherhood – a primary biological difference between the male body and the female body – is/was a marker of dehumanization. Black womanhood became the site of maintenance of the system of dehumanization called slavery. A child became dehumanized and forced into enslavement not based on patrilineal standing but by virtue of having a Black mother. Feminism refused to deal with this germinal difference (and others) in the construction of Black femininity. Thus, Caribbean women use feminism as a philosophical and organizational tool despite not seeing themselves in the theoretical mirror. Is that not self-deprecation?! The working-class women in the Caribbean have constantly called out the negation and rejected labelling themselves feminist even while the 'representatives' of feminism have continued to try to force the doxa onto the masses by virtue of their own privilege, access to power and for narrow career advancement (Ellis 87; Mohammed 23; 24). When I speak of the social construction of gender in the CC, I read all the ways that a legal and societal system deprived the Black female body of its agency and perpetrated systemic and individual damage to those bodies. A critical part of understanding the social construction of gender in the CC then, is accounting for how women have subverted and refused to participate in Western/plantation constructions of society. This book celebrates and legitimates the ways in which Black women changed and redefined performances of gender and femininity to be able to survive the brutality and toxicity of plantation.

Returning to Butler, she and I concur that to construct a generic patriarchy is problematic. I think the answer to her question "is it possible to identify a monolithic as well as a monologic masculinist economy that traverses the array of cultural and historical contexts in which sexual difference takes place"[6] is resoundingly no. While I agree that patriarchy and the relational views about men vis-à-vis women has recognizable, transferable and transnational features, subjugation is region-specific and cultural. Not understanding patriarchy in this way, could result in misinterpreting culture-specific practices that are manifestations of patriarchy and the danger that other actors of patriarchy (such as women who have a vested interest in the maintenance of patriarchy) can cause. In the CC the way that men treat women is not only a consequence of Western patriarchy, but also the result of a specific type of society that germinated around plantation organization of societies and a trauma response.[7] Black men are both affected by the construction of patriarchy and perpetrators of that kind of subjugation. As a minority masculinity they are held outside of power by systemic mechanisms including low or no access to education and career advancement that translates into economic power. Being able to control women and to have multiple women is one of the only symbols of status a Black Caribbean man has.

For CC men to be less invested in the traditional gender roles they rigidly hold onto it will call for a challenge to dominant masculinity. While Black men slavishly uphold that masculinity, they are also subjugated by it and held in a politically disadvantageous position. The right way for Black men to fight that is not to turn their fury on women or children but towards the politourgeoise upholding CC plantation for their narrow gain. The meaning of having a family and being in one must change. Friedrich Engels in his examination of family structure before the plantation proto-capitalist system observed that an important function of family was to mark and claim relations (Engels 58–9). Although he leaves African familial relations out of his analysis, it is relatively well accepted, even from the way family is organized in the Caribbean that our familial concept is expansive. Trauma-informed approaches to family relations can help us to both honour the tradition of what family means in our African tradition and create healthier and safer family relations for the future. In other words, different family relations, grounded in a different relational pattern between heterosexual couples, can move us beyond capitalist/patriarchal notions of family. In terms of their roles as perpetrators of patriarchy, I think the biggest factor in challenging this is to find an appropriate historical and current narrative that opens dialogue between Black men and women. Persisting with using flawed constructions of 'woman' as the point of departure for conversation, will continue to generate inchoate misery in place of healthy relations between men and women.

Suzanne Lafont[8] in her analysis Jamaican family court presented a list of gender beliefs that Caribbean women hold about men and vice versa (96–126). Lafont concludes that a major part of the 'gender war' between Caribbean men and women is grounded in "mutual exploitation" and mistrust among men and women (159). Research and educational opportunities that focus on reformulations of Black femininity can assist Black men to understand Black women both historically and presently. Black men and Black women need to understand that the dysfunction they read as emanating from each other has a clear historical genesis and it can be rewritten to encourage better relations without threat to either male personhood or female personhood. Conversations between Black women and Black men are also not the only ones to be had. Women with a perceived vested interest in patriarchy also do significant damage to other women and that is usually never called out or addressed. CC single mothers, in raising their sons, reproduce and perpetuate several of the toxic formulations of masculinity. This is not the focus of the current argument, but it is one that certainly calls for further elucidation and research.[9]

The third point that Butler makes in *Gender Trouble* useful to my analysis is how the construction of gender rigidly demands separation of masculine and feminine. Butler explains that constructing compulsory heterosexuality necessitates:

> …the production of discrete and asymmetrical opposition between "feminine" and "masculine," where these are understood as expressive attributes of "male" and "female." The cultural matrix through which gender identity has become intelligible requires that certain kinds of "identities" cannot "exist"- that is, those in which gender does not follow form sex and those in which the practices of desire do not "follow" either from sex or gender." (24)

Despite the cogent efforts of Judith Butler and Jack Halberstam to call out conflations in gender theory, there is little said by either about female masculinity that pairs with sexual preference for male intimacy. Given the ways that historical experiences have shaped Black femininity into a particularly masculine femininity this is a major exclusion in feminism and gender theory and only a burgeoning idea in womanism. Although most CC Black men lack the economic means to perform patriarchy, patriarchy offered the only semblance of control many Black men would ever have – not economic or financial stability but brutality over women. Suzanne Lafont explains,

> In many other cultures in which male dominance is significant, male hegemony is supported by the social and economic infrastructure. The men have the finances or power to support their claim to dominance, and

> the women have been oppressed into subordination…Thus, we do not find the overt hostility between the sexes as found in the Caribbean. (4)

Many CC men, even the ones who have not much more than the hair on their heads, want to be brutal and to control women (who are often at least self-sufficient). After independence men consolidated the political and juridical power they gained for the subjugation of women. At the same time that compulsory heterosexualization was causing erasure for queer genders and sexualities it was causing friction and conflict in Caribbean gender negotiations. What I define as compulsory heterosexuality is not about whether a woman has sex with men. It is, more importantly, a forced removal of agency to resist subjugation and oppression JUST because a woman desires men sexually. To pair biological heterosexuality with gender butchness is to reclaim standing. It allows a woman to demand partner accountability and safety in the experience of partnerships with the opposite sex. It is time and attention to disrupt patriarchal views and discourses as 'natural' and resistance against "…reproductive, and medicojuridical hegemonies" (Butler 26). All female masculinity is not queer. Queer studies should have convinced us by now that sexuality is not glibly chosen. However, being born heterosexual is not 'giving in' to male suppression. A woman can have sex with men and reject the aspects of compulsory heterosexuality that are hegemonic and misogynistic.

Femininity as it appears in general use is always a synonym for female femininity – the kind necessary to legitimate patriarchy. However, Black women's experiences of Transatlantic dehumanization shed light on how Diasporic women's femininities underwent change as a result of colonialization. Hilary Beckles[10] in the book *Natural Rebels* explains that slave masters in Barbados soon deduced that female labour could perform the same tasks as male labour in the plantation enterprise due to their leadership and experience in agriculture based on their roles in Africa (7–9). It was an added incentive that African women were sold into slavery cheaper than men. The implications of this are important for gender relations in the Barbados and I argue the broader CC. It is ahistorical to believe Black women needed feminism to teach them to be strong and self-sufficient. Their experiences of slavery outlined in Chapter 1 made them so. Caribbean women have always worked outside of the household and they were never afforded male protection. Beckles notes that field women captives were expected to produce equally with male counterparts (*Natural Rebels* 31). Relationships between Black men and Black women in Barbados and the CC were never established on the premise of women as 'gentle sex' who needed to be cared and provided for. Due to their lot as 'beasts of burden'[11] to be made maximally productive in the plantation enterprise, their lived experience made Black masculine femininity a legitimate option in comparison to other types of femininity in other socioracial contexts.

In addition, to the expectation that they work equally to men in the plantation enterprise sexual abuse was pervasive as a method of dehumanization and punishment of Black women. Beckles writes that Black women in the ships brought to the colonial holds were exposed to:

> …heightened sexual vulnerability and the abuse that characterized the passage experience. Undoubtedly, rape and other forms of physical and emotional violence at the hands of the white crew shaped the consciousness of African women in the passage, and **established psychological structures that dictated subsequent attitudes to life on the estates**. Many women arrived in the Caribbean already impregnated by ship's crews… Significantly, then, African women's consciousness as they became sugar plantation field hands was shaped by their experiences in Africa and the Atlantic. (*Natural Rebels* 27) (my emphasis added)

Beckles does not articulate what the "psychological structures" activated were, but I am suggesting that masculine femininity was a tool of agency used by Black women to mitigate and manage the trauma of rape and sexual violence. I am not reading Black women's adjustment and approach to sexuality as pathological in any way. There was and still is no benefit to Black women to need saving! Who will save them? Black men who subjugate them in fighting their own liberation battle? White women who are often more harmful to Black women in workplace situations than white men? Since it brought and still brings no reward Black women, they cultivated a womanhood that suited the realities. Butler is unhappy with the social construction of gender that removes agency from (female) bodies and makes them things that gender can just be acted upon (12). While I do not disagree with where she takes her refutation, my own focus in this book rests more with the agency that (female) bodies have to re/negotiate gender even with acceptance that there are social factors present in gender construction. That gender is socially constructed can be a liberatory fact.

The trauma of sexual violence did not disappear with legal emancipation as Maude's case study in Chapter Two reminds. Aishah Simmons traces sexual violence through the experience of Black women even within some of the most celebratory moments including the Civil Rights Movement (172). She also speaks on the importance of support and programming that helps women to overcome sexual violence and live their lives as whole and healed women (171). None of this healing work or healing space was readily available to the Caribbean foremothers who experienced the brutality and torture of the plantation experience and the subsequent normalization of (sexual) violence against Black women. Many of them have not recovered from this personal experience and the best many of them could do and did was to raise future generations of Caribbean women who in our negotiation of femininity employ strategies that mitigate against vulnerability and falling prey to sexual violence.

The question as to whether these strategies work or not is not the focus here. I accept that Black women – whether Butch or not and Black men have healing to do by virtue of our historical experiences. Butch heterosexuality is more complex than simply requesting an inversion of gender roles from men (hooks, *The Will to Change* 117). I am not asking for unequal power relations to be inverted. This is not about retribution. The point simply is that Black women's experiences are germinal to theorizing social constructions of gender, especially to interpreting social construction of gender as agency. They have reconstituted their womanhood into resistance praxis that culls (individualistic) patriarchal social systems. PPC is a present tense not a past or historical explanation. Despite continued decolonization efforts such as Barbados's move to Republican status in November 2021, the treatment of women and girls reveals a kind of gendered, unequal citizenship status. (Black) Women's inequality is a palpable result of PPC. Much as it was during the eighteenth century and legal emancipation, plantation patriarchal culture remains prohibitive to the enjoyment of freedom in the Caribbean (Fog Olwig, "Cultural Complexity after Freedom" 101). While Fog Olwig placed a conjoiner between 'plantation' and 'patriarchal', I remove it because the two always appear together and the one upholds the other in the context of the CC social matrix. Women and girls are twice affected. Several writers have underscored the rigid social structure of plantation systems and their problematic nature (Best 4–5; Fog Olwig, "Introduction: Emancipation and Its Consequences" 3–6; Thomas, *Political Life in the Wake of the Plantation* 212–20).

This rigid structure holds women in place both in relation to men and also in relation to other women.[12] Women's relationships with each other – the levels of toxicity and oppressiveness – must also be reviewed in discussing CC gender relations. I explored this in relation to women's organizing in Chapter Three. Colourism and class privilege have been overlooked in term of the damage that they generate among women. The Victorian expectations of womanhood which became desirable norms after legal emancipation have been another way that women have been hemmed in by plantation society. The hatred for Black women and Black motherhood was reinvented in Victorian expectations of female 'goodness' in the CC. For instance, while it has never been cultural for men to stand by Black women during pregnancy and motherhood, Black women have been chastised relentlessly for being promiscuous and for having children with multiple partners. Black women's inability to earn a living wage as occupiers of the bottom-most identity in a plantation hierarchical structure has also been used against them. Many have sexual relationships with men as a survival mechanism and then are painted as 'tricksters' or 'charlatans'. Karen Fog Olwig explains:

> The first cultural tradition to be established on the island is that connected with the development during the 1600s of a colonial society based on plantations. It is associated with the British settlers who came from the

> hierarchical rural society of early modern England. Where inferiors found their place in an occupational, hierarchical family under the headship of a patriarch. In the West Indies, the patriarch evolved into a slave master who personally or through a manager headed a large workforce of slaves (SIC), most of whom occupied such a lowly position in the hierarchy that they had no social identity except as their owner's property. **This patriarchal system was not merely economic, however; for it was associated with familial traditions and institutions that, in various permutations, presented the under class – first white servants and then black slaves (SIC) – with possibilities for expressing a cultural identity of their own making within an otherwise oppressive plantation system.** (my emphasis added) ("Cultural Complexity after Freedom" 104)

When the CC became independent, patriarchs changed colour from a white massa or overseer to a Black member of the political elite or professional classes. The major expansion that I make to Fog Olwig's concept of PPC is that whereas the institutions were controlled by colonial forces before independence after they are controlled by the politourgeoisie and the individualistic patriarchal status quo. The men become more powerful after independence and the women become more powerless. In Chapter Two, matrilineality and the care and control of children are analysed to show the shifts of power. Despite any gains made in switching traditional gender roles, the reality is CC women perform and negotiate gender inside PPC.

CC societies remain some of the most oppressive and dangerous to the existence of Black women. Despite changes in law, what is written in statute is far different from the everyday experience of women and girls and there is a barrier of complicity and protection among men and state functions such as the judiciary. CAP 130A, The Domestic Violence Protection Order Act is reviewed in Chapter Three to explore the gap between law and practice. Black women who sleep with men should not be dismissed as automatically supportive of masculine domination and oppression. I combined intellectual argument with case study and my lived experience of coming into womanhood to point out that Caribbean women have always assumed characteristics that are categorized as 'masculine' such as autonomy, independence and choice over who they have sexual relations with. Notwithstanding, perhaps legitimately, the question of why I choose the term 'butch' as the modifier for this type of gender identity can be tabled. Jack Halberstam's *Female Masculinity* is a canonical work on female masculinity. Jack ably expounds key theoretical and representational issues of female masculinity. Halberstam focuses specifically on butchness as a type of female masculinity while at the same time showing that butch sexuality can be performed multiple ways.

For instance, Halbertam discusses the stone butch who gives pleasure during sex but declines receiving it (123). The fact that 'Butch' appears as a modifier with another word to describe the sexuality practised by the butch is proof that butch is not a sexuality but rather a gender orientation. There is no reason why the modifier Butch cannot qualify the referent heterosexual. Halberstam highlights the fact that there are multiple heterosexualities and a way in which women's work or social positioning (urban or rural in Halberstam's example and positioning in a plantation society in mine) can shape the performance of heterosexuality (51–7). Jack clearly makes room in female masculinity in for heterosexual women although he is honest that his project does not explicate it:

> ...There are likely to be many examples of masculine women in history who had no interest in same-sex sexuality. While it is not within the scope of this book to do so, there is probably a lively history of the masculine heterosexual woman to be told, a history, moreover that must be buried by the bundling of all female masculinities into lesbian identity (57).

This book used a conceptual historical approach to provide a glimpse into masculine femininity and the experience of Black women in plantation society. I hope it is only the beginning of many years of debate and research. I wholeheartedly agree with Halberstam that, "...the general concept of female masculinity has its uses for heterosexual women" (268). More visibility is needed for female masculinity, especially where it occurs with the sexual identity of women who sleep with men.

Butch heterosexuality or other formulations may have been eschewed before now for multiple reasons. For one, as bell hooks notes, sexism and racial oppression are baked into Black socialization. This stopped women from being too concerned with womanhood and how it was made (*Ain't I A Woman* 1). Black women spent a lot of time fighting to be seen as good as, and just like white women. Compulsory heterosexuality made women who could be shielded under the privilege of heterosexuality have no incentive to move beyond that to claim something as taboo as butchness. While I am not trying to create a monolithic view of understanding Black femininity in this contemporary moment, I am trying to expand language and approaches to understanding Black femininity. Masculine women can now be Butch and free! If I am completely transparent my motivation in writing this book has naught to do with how society sees me and everything to do with how I see myself and other women and greater access to support from my Black Kings. This is an unapologetic explanation of myself.

When I use 'butch' to modify the type of sexuality I am writing about here I am amplifying butchness as a rejection of patriarchal and social constructions of womanhood that demand seamless adherence between feminine femininity and sexual desire for men. Butch heteros will not participate in patriarchy. While a Butch hetero will allow penetration as a part of sexual desire and performance, they do not allow it as a feature of trauma-informed partnership. As a Butch hetero identifying person, I do not see heterosexuality as the marker of 'natural' sexuality just the one that I find pleasure in. Emotional diminution and an overall loss of power or independence is not accepted to be with a male partner. The Butch hetero is closed to patriarchal constructions of femininity that renders women capable of absorbing abuse and emotional harm to be in intimate partnership. She is open to male aesthetics in dress both because it is practical and stylish. She finds little use for good manners, frills, stockings and high heels. While she is open to heterosexual sex inclusive of vaginal penetration this is for her pleasure and is a part of a loop where she both gives and gains pleasure. Sex is never linked to monetary reward for her and she may even enjoy being the breadwinner in her relation or at least a financial aid to her partner. Butch heteros reel against any form of sexualization in the public or workplace space for example but remains very open to pleasing and being pleased by a sexual partner of her choosing. But heterosexuality is an alternative to Victorian performances of womanhood that never suited the CC Black woman. White femininity is not replicated by the masses of CC Black women because its purpose is partly to create the type of woman a patriarch needs to be a patriarch and Black women were never invested in assisting their own subjugation.[13]

Butch heterosexuality as a performance of womanhood is a legitimate contemporary possibility for the Caribbean. Our foremothers' hard work and resistance have resulted in more financial independence for women. Our foremothers were the innovators of strong femininity but, in many cases they lacked the full autonomy and economic framework to enact it as much as modern CC women can. The traditional practice of Caribbean women not to get married and to maintain singleness is a powerful personal manifestation of a profound resistance philosophy – one centuries old in the CC and now en vogue elsewhere. Butchness also provides possibilities for us to love each other differently as women. Butches are women who love women, sexually and otherwise. This can help us to heal the divisions and wounds among us as Black women. Women can support, care for and relate to each other just as a consequence of our shared and different realities. The women's movement in the Caribbean has not encouraged this revolution and it is necessary and needed. As much as I am focusing on relationships between woman and men, I am also cultivating space for a different type of understanding of femininity that is safer – woman to woman. Butches after all, are deeply invested in female love. Women can benefit from woman-to-woman love. Women can and should love each other. Women can and should romance each other. Women have loved each other. Women need to love each other to heal and grow.

My granny's home, where I grew up, was one where Black women were outside of, beyond, not in relationship with any kind of traditional gender or sexuality markers and that is not new or uncomfortable. It has always been our reality more than not as Black women. Despite our differences we have all continued to be in relative community with each other. In many ways the confluence of Blackness and gender has always made us 'other' and misjudged. That is my tribe – that is my people. Black women are survivors. After generations and generations of systemic and individual brutality, Black women have constructed a femininity that took account of their historical and social experiences of PPC. Due to the rigours of the work they performed, first on the plantation, and then as an under or last class in plantation societies, to secure basic survival they have adapted their femininity in a way that has been obscured by mainstream gender theory and feminism. Black Caribbean men have been fed myths of patriarchy they have never truly lived, but they invest in their myth because of its potential for elusive power. They experience Black femininity as offensive, emasculating and burdensome. Black men are especially offended by female masculinity because of their own fragile hold on positioning in male masculine structures.[14] Feminists celebrate the 'success' of their movement but the true test of how far we have gotten with equality is that butch heteros as bearers of a kind of female masculinity still struggle to find partners.

Black (Caribbean) women have always protested a feminism that abhors their partnerships with men. Endorsing butch heterosexuality can offer important answers not just for understanding Black femininity but as Butler calls for, closing the gap between femininity and masculinity in such a way that expands important gender notions and allows "...subversive sites of their convergence and resignification" (44). Butch heterosexuality is a challenge to and not compulsory heterosexuality. Butch heterosexuality is a disruptive gender/sexual orientation. It proves Butler's assertion that "...the regulatory fictions of sex and gender are themselves multiple contested sites of meaning, then the very multiplicity of their construction holds out the possibility of a disruption of their univocal posturing" (44). I suggest that much of what I have contemplated in this book has been overlooked because of the degree to which Black (Caribbean) femininity was overlooked in the construction of the 'woman' that became the subject of feminism.

I endorse Halberstram's reading of masculinity as a dialectic,

> ...male and female masculinities are constantly involved in an ever-shifting pattern of influence. We tend to identify the pattern as moving only in one direction, rather than seeing the possibilities of an active matrix of exchange between male and female masculinities (276).

It is possible for there to be healthy equilibrium, and partnership and Black love between man and woman – if I can be accepted for my history and trauma, agency and resilience. Perhaps this will be a hard pill for Caribbean men to swallow but here are two doses of reality that hopefully make it easier. First this book and several more like it and peripheral to it prove that Black

Caribbean women were never hopeless, helpless or subjugated to men. Second, again in Halberstam's words because they are economical and sensible,

> I do not believe that we are moving steadily toward a genderless society or even that this is a utopia to be desired, but I do believe that a major step toward gender parity, and one that has been grossly overlooked, is the cultivation of female masculinity (272).

Is it more useful for a Black man to love a helpless woman or is it better for him to invest care in a survivor who can match and return his energy and even be a portal to his own healing? Halberstam again:

> If gender has become a battleground at this time, it is worth asking who fights the battle, who receives wounds and bears scars, who dies? The gender struggles, furthermore, has a way of collapsing gender and sexuality because for gender outlaws, their gender bending is often read as the outlaw sign of an aberrant sexuality (118–19).

Here I am King.

Notes

1 Commentaries on the speech available online including (Sourjourner Truth Ain't I am Woman) by the National Parks Service, US Department of the Interior.

2 The title for the chapter and further refinement of the idea also developed during the weekly gatherings of the Research Innovation Committee, University of Guelph between December 2022 and February 2023.

3 Butler argues convincingly that feminism depends problematically on juridical formulations of its main category of analysis, woman (2–4). One of the major issues with the construction of woman by feminism is that it has resulted in erasure of non-white women including black women – the focus of this chapter. Butler uses the term feminist critique in the original quote but exactly for her explanation of the problems with definitions and formulations in feminism, I replace the word 'feminist' with 'womanist' in a desire to recognize the dangers of feminism and not to replicate them.

4 If I do not adhere to gender binaries, which should I adhere to academic ones? See the article I wrote on alternative approaches to feminism such as the Caribbean indigenous concept of conscience. Noted I argue women's organizer Andaiye embeds conscience in the work she does with the formation of Red Thread in Guyana and her Caribbean-wide nationalist agitation (Hinds Myrie 4–7).

5 See Halberstam for his discussion of how Black woman bodies are already excluded from proper femininity due to our propensity to be more muscular than other women (Halberstam xiii; 271).

6 Butler 2007 (18).

7 For years CC women have fought to remain in relation to their male folks even as they fight for their own liberation because they recognize that Black men themselves are also oppressed and affected/damaged by the structure of patriarchy.

8 I think that Lafont's analysis is very useful and although it was done in 1995 is still very relevant to understanding the performance of gender by men and women and the culture of the family court in the CC. The two major contentions that I have with her work is how she glosses or underplays the role of violence in matters that reach the family court and her reading of her analysis as only applying to the 'lower' class of Jamaican society. The analysis is not class-based and it outlines features that a common to family structures at all levels of CC society. Her work again highlights the differences between native analysis and foreign analysis in CC knowledge making.

9 There is a dearth of (current) research on the relationships between single mothers and their children in the CC. My interaction with male perpetrators of domestic and intimate partner violence over my career as a practising advocate reveals a pattern of motherly support for and complicity with their sons. The result of this is that women are an active part in maintaining cycles of abuse and oppressive behaviour in the Caribbean context. Some of the research available on these topics are Barry Chaevannes' *Learning to be a Man* and Eugene Brody's *Sex, Contraception, and Motherhood in Jamaica.*

10 Beckles does make the point that preference for female enslaved Africans was a particularly Barbadian phenomenon and there are cases to show the opposite pertained in other territories of the CC. The preference for females also fluctuated based on where in the cycle of production a plantation was.

11 Hilary Beckles (55) attributes the use of this descriptor of field women to William Dickson.

12 See Hilary Beckles "Sex and Gender in the Historiography of Caribbean Slavery" on how the experience of plantation disrupts and shapes the relationships among women (131).

13 See Judith Butler (56). Women have to be active participants in patriarchy in order for it to work. I contend that this is a major contention between Black women and Black men because Black women have never been helpless or happy participants in upholding patriarchy. Since Black men's access to patriarchy is very dependent on controlling women they have always seen this as an affront.

14 See Halberstam (40–41).

Works Cited

Adojoh-Davoh, Valerie Delali. "Patriarch and Cultural values in Nineteenth- and Twentieth-Century Ghana." *Negotiating Patriarchy and Gender in Africa: Discourses, Practices, and Policies*. Ed. Egodi Uchendu, and Ngozi Edeagu. Maryland: Lexington Books, 2021. 109–21. Print.

Allahar, Anton. "Charisma and Populism: Theoretical Reflections on Leadership and Legitimacy." *Caribbean Charisma: Reflections on Leadership, Legitimacy and Populist Politics*. Ed. Anton Allahar. Kingston: Ian Randle Publishers, 2001. 1–32. Print.

Allsop, Richard. *Dictionary of Caribbean English Usage*. Kingston: U of West Indies P, 2003. Print.

Andaiye. "The Regional Women's Movement." *The Point Is to Change the World: Selected Writings of Andaiye*. Ed. Alissa Trotz. London: Pluto Press, 2020. 37–46. Print.

Baptist, Edward. *The Half Has Never Been Told: Slavery and the Making of American Capitalism*. New York: Basic Books, 2014. Print.

Beckford, George. "Plantation Society: Toward a General Theory of Caribbean Society."*Caribbean Cultural Thought: From Plantation to Diaspora*. Ed. Hume Yanique Kamguisha and Aaron. Ian Randle Publishers: Print, 2013. 109–19.

Beckles, Hilary. *A History of Barbados: From Amerindian Settlement to Caribbean Single Market*. New York: Cambridge U P, 2006.

Beckles, Hilary. *Chattel House Blues Making of a Democratic Society in Barbados: From Clement Payne to Owen Arthur*. Kingston: Ian Randle Publishers, 2004.

Beckles, Hilary. *Natural Rebels: A Social History of Enslaved Black Women in Barbados*. New Brunswick: Rutgers University Press, 1989.

Beckles, Hilary. "Perfect Property: Enslaved Black Women in the Caribbean."*Confronting Power; Theorizing Gender*. Ed. Eudine Barriteau. Kingston: Ian Randle Publishers, 2003. 142–58. Print.

Beckles, Hilary. "Sex and Gender in the Historiography of Caribbean Slavery."*Engendering History: Caribbean Women in Historical Perspective*. Ed. Verene Shepherd, Bridget Brereton and Barbara Bailey. Jamaica: Ian Randal, 1995. 125–40. Print.

Best, Lloyd. "On the Teaching of Economics." *Essays on The Theory of Plantation Economy: A Historical and Institutional Approach to Caribbean Economic Development*. Ed. Best Llyod and Kari Polanyi Levitt. Jamaica: U of the West Indies P, 2009. 1–7. Print.

Brathwaite, Kamau. *The Development of Creole Society in Jamaica 1770–1820*. Kingston: Ian Randle Publishers, 2005. Print.

Bryant, Courtney. *Erotic Definance: Womanism, Freedom and Resistance*. Minneapolis: Fortress Press, 2023. Print.

Burnard, Trevor and Garrigus, John. *The Plantation Machine: Atlantic Capitalism in French Saint-Domingue and British Jamaica*. Philadelphia: U of Pennsylvania P, 2016. Print.

Burnard, Trevor. *Mastery, Tyranny, & Desire*. North Carolina: U of North Carolina P, 2004. print.

Butler, Judith. *Gender Trouble*. New York: Routledge, 2007. Print.

CARICOM Community. *CARICOM Caribbean Community: A Community for All*. 2025. https://caricom.org/caricom-ten-point-plan-for-reparatory-justice/. 17 March 2025.

Cassidy, F. G. and Robert LePage. *Dictionary of Jamaican English*. Kingston: U of the West Indies Press, 2002. Print.

Chevannes, Barry. *Betwixt and Between: Explorations in an African Caribbean Mindscape*. Kingston: Ian Randle Publishers, 2006. Print.

Chevannes, Barry. *Learning to Be a Man*. Kingston: Ian Randle Publishers, 2001. Print.

Clarke, Edith. *My Mother Who Fathered Me: A Study of the Families in Three Selected Communities of Jamacia*. Kingston: U of the West Indies P, 1999. Print.

Conti, Paul. *Trauma: The Invisible Pandemic How Trauma works and How to Heal from It*. Colorado: Sounds True Publishing, 2021. Print.

Cummins, James. *Barack-Yard Dwellers*. Port-of-Spain: U of West Indies, 2004. Print.

DeGruy, Joy. *Post Traumatic Slave Syndrome*. Milwaukie, Oregon: Uptone Press, 2017.

Doddington, David. "Manhood, Sex and Power in Antebellum Slave Societies."*Sexuality and Slavery: Reclaiming Intimate Histories in the Americas*. Ed. Daina Ramey Berry and Leslie Harris. Georgia: U of Georgia P, 2018. 145–58. Print.

Downes, Aviston. "Gender and the Elementary Teaching Service in Barbados, 1880–1960." *Confronting Power, Theorizing Gender: Interdisciplinary Perspectives in the Caribbean*. Ed. Eudine Barriteau. Kingston: U of West Indies P, 2003. 303–32. Print.

Downing, Antonio Michael. *Saga Boy: My Life of Blackness and Becoming*. Canada: Penguin Random House, 2021. Print.

Downs, Jim. "When the Present Is Past: Writing the History of Sexuality and Slavery." *Sexuality and Slavery: Reclaiming Intimate Histories in the Americas*. Ed. Daina Ramey Berry and Harris, Leslie. Georgia: U of Georgia P, 2018. 189–204. print.

Drew, Benjamin. *The Narratives of Fugitive Slaves*. Toronto: Prospero Books, 2000. Print.

Dunkley, D. A. *Women and Resistance int He Early Rastafarian Movement*. Louisiana: Lousiana U P, 2021. Print.

Dunn, Richard. *Sugar & Slaves: The Rise of the Planter Class in the English West Indies, 1624–1713*. North Carolina: U of Carolina P, 1972. Print.

Ellis, Patricia. *Women, Gender & Development in the Caribbean: Reflections and Projections*. Jamaica: Ian Randal Publishers, 2003. Print.

Engels, Friedrich. *The Origins of the Family, Private Property and the State*. London: Penguin Classics, 1972. Print.

Flynn Bruey, Veronica. "Introduction."*Patriarchy and Gender in Africa*. Ed. Veronica Flynn Bruey. Maryland: Lexington Books, 2021. 1–12. Print.

Fog Olwig, Karen. "Cultural Complexity after Freedom: Nevis and Beyond."*Small Islands, Large Questions – Society, Culture and Resistance in the Post-Emancipation Caribbean*. Ed. Karen Fog Olwig. Britain: Ftrank Cass & Co. Ltd, 1995. 100–20. Print.

Fog Olwig, Karen. "Introduction: Emancipation and Its Consequences." *Small Islands, Large Questions: Society, Culture and Resistance in the Post Emancipation Caribbean*. Ed. Karen Fog Olwig. England: Frank Cass and Co., 1995. 3–6. Print.

Foster, Thomas. *Rethinking Rufus: Sexual Violations of Enslaved Men*. Georgia: U of Georgia P, 2019. print.

Foster, Thomas. "The Sexual Abuse of Black Men under American Slavery." *Sexuality and Slavery: Reclaiming Intimate Histories in the Americas*. Ed. Daina Ramey Berry and Leslie Harris. Georgia: U of Georgia P, 2018. 124–44. Print.

Fuentes, Marisa. "Reading the Specter of Racialized Gender in Eighteenth-Century Bridgetown, Barbados." *Seexuality and Slavery: Reclaiming Intimate Histories in the Americas*. Ed. Daina Ramey Berry and Leslie Harris. Georgia: U of Georgia P, 2018. 49–70. Print.

Givan, Norman. "Foreword." *The Theory of Plantation Economy: A Historical and Institutional Approach to Caribbean Economic Development*. Ed. LLoyd Best and Kari Levitt. Mona: U of West Indies P, 2009. xvii–xxiii. print.

Glymph, Thavolia. *Out of the House of Bondage: The Transformation of the Plantation Household.* New York: Cambridge U P, 2008. print.

Gottlieb, Karla. "Queen Nanny of the Jamaican Maroons: A Study of Women's Leadership in the Caribbean." *Women in Caribbean Politics*. Ed. Cynthia Barrow-Giles. Kingston: Ian Randle Publishing, 2011. 3–13. Print.

Gramsci, Antonio. "Socialism and Culture." *Gramsci: Pre-Prison Writings*. Ed. Richard Bellamy. New York: Cambridge U P, 1994. 8–14. Print.

Green, Cecelia. "The Abandoned Lower Class of Females: Class, Gender and Penal Discipline in Barbados 1875–1929." *Comparative Studies in Society and History* 53.1 (2011): 144–79. Print.

Gregg, Veronica Marie. "Preface."*Caribbean Women: An Anthology of Non-Fiction Writing 1890–1980*. Ed. Veronica Marie Gregg. Indiana: U of Notre Dame P, 2005. xiii–xxii. Print.

Halberstam, Jack. *Female Masculinity*. Durham: Duke U P, 2018. print.

Hall, Catherine. *Civilising Subjects: Metropole and Colony in the English imagination 1830–1867*. Chicago: U Chicago P, 2002. Print.

Hall, Douglas. *In Miserable Slavery*. Kingston: U West Indies P, 1999. Print.

Hamad, Ruby. *White Tears/Brown Scars: How White Feminism BEtrays Women of Colour.* New York: Catapult, 2019. 166–75. Print.

Hamilton, Jill. *Women of Barbados: Amerindian Era to Mid 20th Centurey*. Bridgetown: Letchworth Press, c. 1981.

Hartman, Saidiya. *Lose Your Mother: A Journey along the Atlantic Slave Route*. New York: Farrar, Straus and Giroux, 2007. print.

Henry, Paget. *Caliban's Reason: Introducing Afro-Caribbean Philosophy*. New York: Routledge, 2000. Print.

Henry, Paget. "Caribbean Dependence in the Phase of Informatic Capitalism." *The Thought of New World: The Quest for Decolonization*. Ed. Brian Meeks and Norman Girvan. Kingston: Ian Randle Publishers, 2010. 172–205. Print.

Hinds Myrie, Marsha and Anya Lorde. "Plantocratic Patriarchal Culture, Violence against Women and Girls and the Failures of the Global Heralth Ststem: An Interview with Marsha Hinds Myrie and Anya Lorde." *Health Sociology Review* 33.2 (2024): 1–13. Online. https://cls-uk.org.uk/wp-content/uploads/2022/12/women.pdf.

Hinds Myrie, Marsha. "Women and Caribbean Socialism: If We Are for Liberation the Woman Question Is a Legitimate Question." *Cutlass: Women and the Left in the Caribbean* (2022): 2–15. https://cls-uk.org.uk/wp-content/uploads/2022/12/women.pdf0.

hooks, bell. *Ain't I A Woman: Black Wowmen and Feminism*. Boston: Pluto Press, 1982. Print.
hooks, bell. *All about Love: New Visions*. New York: Harper Perennial, 2000. Print.
hooks, bell. *The Will to Change: Men, Masculinity, and Love*. New York: Washington Square Press, 2004. Print.
hooks, bell. *We Real Cool: Black Men and Masculinity*. New York: Routeledge, 2004. print.
Hudson-Weems, Clenora. *Africana Womanism: Reclaiming Ourselves*. New York: Routledge, 2020. Print.
Iantaffi, Alex. *Gender Trauma: Healing Cultural, Social, and Historical Gendered Trauma*. London: Jessica Kingsley Publishers, 2021. Print.
Jackson, Regina and Saira Rao. *White Women: Everything you Already Know about Your Own Racism and How to Do Better*. New York: Pengiun Books, 2022. Print.
Jemmott, Jenny. *Ties That Bind: The Black Family in Post-Slavery Jamacia, 1834–1882*. Jamaica: U West Indies Press, 2015. Print.
Johnson, Jessica Marie. *Wicked Flesh: Black WOmen, Intimacy and Freedom in the Atlantic World*. Philadelphia: U of Pennsylvania P, 2020. Print.
Keating, AnaLouise. *Transformation Now!* Chicago: U of Illinois P, 2013. Print.
Knight, Franklin. "The Caribbean in the 1930s." *General History of the Caribbean*. Ed. Bridget Brereton. London: UNESCO Publishing, 2004. 42–141. Print.
Knight, Franklin. *The Caribbean: The Genesis of a Fragmented Nationalism*. New York: Oxford U Press, 2012. Print.
LaFont, Suzanne. *The Emergence of an Afro-Caribbean Legal Traidtion: Gender Relations and Family Courts in Kingston, Jamaica*. Maryland: Austin and Winfield Publishers, 1995. Print.
Laws of Barbados. "CAP 130A Domestic Violence (Protection Orders) Act." Bridgetown, 13 February 1992. Print.
Lerner, Gerda. *The Creation of Patriarchy*. Oxford: Oxford U P, 1986. Print.
Lewis, Linden. "Exploring the Intersections of Gender, Sexuality, and Culture in the Caribbean: An Introduction."*The Cuture of Gender and Sexuality in the Caribbean*. Ed. Linden Lewis. Florida: U of Florida Press, 2003. 1–21. Print.
Lorde, Audre. *Zami: A New Spelling of My Name*. New York: Crossing Press, 1982. Print.
Mathurin-Mair, Lucille. "Reluctant Matriarchs." *Caribbean Cultural Thought: From Plantation to Diaspora*. Ed. Yanique Hume and Aaron Kamuguisha. Kingston: Ian Randle Publishers, 2013. 130–4. Print.
Mauro, Anne. *The Colonialization of Black Sexualities: A Clinical Guide to Relearning and Healing*. New York: Routledge, 2024.
Miller, Errol. *Marginalization of the Black Male: Insights from the Development of the Teaching Profession*. Kingston: Montrose Printery, 1986. Print.
Mohammed, Patricia and Perkins, Althea. *Caribbean Women at the Crossroads: The Paradox of Motherhood among Women of Barbados, St. Lucia and Dominica*. Kingston: U West Indies Press, 1999. Print.
Mohammed, Patricia. "Towards Indigenous Feminist Theorizing in the Caribbean." *Feminist Review* No.59 (1998): 6–33.
Moore, Brian and Johnson, Michele. *Neither Led nor Driven: Contesting British Cultural Imperialism in Jamaica, 1865–1920*. Kingston: U W I Press, 2004. Print.
Morgan, Jennifer. "Partus Sequitar Ventrem: Law, Race and Reproduction in Colonial Slavery." *Small Axe* 55 (2018): 1–17. Print.

Nash, Gary. "Foreword." *Sugar & Slaves: The Rise of the Planter Class in the English West Indies, 1694–1713*. Ed. Richard Dunn. North Carolina: U of North Carolina P, 2000. xiii–xx. Print.

Onyeani, Chika. *Capitalist Nigger: The Road to Success a Spider Web Doctrine*. Johannesburg: Jonathan Ball Publishers, 2006. print.

OO v BK and Another. No. [2023] CCJ 10 (AJ) BB. Caribbean Court of Justice. 28 July 2023. https://opac.ccj.org/GeniePlus/Portal/Default.aspx?lang=en-US&p_AAAAIR1=AAAAIZ&d=d.

Pateman, Carole. *The Sexual Contract*. California: Stanford U P, 2018. Print.

Patterson, Orlando. *The Sociology of Slavery*. Cambridge: Polity Press, 2022. Print.

Phillips, Layli. "Introduction – Womanism: On Its Own." *The Womanist Reader*. Ed. Phillips Layli. New York: Routeledge, 2006. xix–iv. Print.

Pierre, Jemima. *Teh Predicament of Blackness: Postcolonial Ghana and the Politics of Race*. Chicago: U of Chicago P, 2013. Print.

Reddock, Reddock. *Women Labour and Politics in Trinidad and Tobago: A History*. New Jersey: Zed Books, 1994.

Reddock, Rhoda. "Introduction." *Women, Labour & Politics in Trinidad and Tobago: A History*. Ed. Rhoda Reddock. London: Zed Books, 1994. 1–10. Print.

Richardson, Bonham. *Panama Money in Barbados, 1900–1920*. Knoxville: U Tennessee Press, 1985. Print.

Robertson, Glory. "Pictoral Sources for Ninteenth-Century Women's History: Drees as a Mirror of Attitudes to Women." *Engendering History: Caribbean Women in Historical Perspective*. Ed. Verene Shepherd et al. Kinsgton: Ian Randle Publishers, 1995. 111–22. Print.

Rodney, Walter. *How Europe Underdeveloped Africa*. London: Verso Publishing, 2018. Print.

Saini, Angela. *The Patriarchs: The Origins of Inequality*. Boston: Beacon Press, 2023. Print.

Sen, Gita and Caren Grown. *Development, Crises and Alternative Visions*. New York: Monthly Review Press, 1987. Print.

Sheller, Mimi. *Citizenship from Below: Erotic Agency and Caribbean Freedom*. Durham: Duke U P, 2012. Print.

Shorter Brown, Yvonne. *Dead Woman Pickney: A Memoir of Childhood in Jamaica*. Ontario: Wilfred Laurier Press, 2022. Print.

Silvera, Makeda. "Man Royal and Sodomites: Some Thoughts on the Invisibility of Afro-Caribbean Lesbians." *Feminist Studies* 18.3 (1992): 521–32. Online.

Simmons, Aishah. "The War against Black Women, and the Making of No." *Color of Violence: The INCITE! Women of Color against Violence*. North Carolina: Duke U P, 2016. 170–8. online.

Smith, Raymond. *The Negro Family in British Guiana*. New York: Routledge, 1956. Print.

Spencer Gibbs, Rose. *Island of Plantations*. Independently published, 2022. print.

Spooner, Mary. "Protecting Victims of Domestic Violence in Caribbean Communities." *Journal of Immigration and Refugee Services* 2.3-4 (2009): 1536–2957. https://doi.org/10.1300/J191v02n03_08.

Stevenson, Brenda. "What's Love Got to Do with It: Concubinage and Enslaved Women and Girls in the Antebellum South." *Sexuality and Slavery: Reclaiming Intimate Histories in the Americas*. Ed. Daina Ramey Berry and Leslie Harris. Georgia: U of Georgia P, 2018. 159–88. Print.

Thomas, Deborah. *Exceptional Violence: Embodied Citizenship in Transnational Jamaica*. Durham: Duke U P, 2011. Print.

Thomas, Deborah. *Political Life in the Wake of the Plantation: Sovereignty, Witnessing, Repair*. Pennsylvania: Duke U. P, 2019.

Trouillot, Michel- Rolph. "The Caribbean Region: An Open Frontier in Antropological Theory." *Annual Review of Antropology* 21 (1992): 19–42. Print.

Van Der Kolk, Bessel. *The Body Keeps the Score: Brain, Mind and Body in the Healing of Trauma*. New York: Penguin Books, 2014. Print.

Vasconcellos, Colleen. *Slavery, Childhood, and Abolition in Jamaica 1788–1838*. Georgia: U of Georgia P, 2015. Print.

Walcott, Rinaldo. *The Long Emancipation Toward Black Freedom*. North Carolina: Duke U P, 2021.

Walker, Alice. "Womanist."*The Womanist Reader*. Ed. Layli Phillips. New York: Routledge, 2006. 19. Print.

Watson, Hilbourne. "Errol Barrow (1920–1987) The Social Construction of Colonial and Post-Colonial Charismatic Political Leadership in Bartbados." *Caribbean Charisma: Reflections on Leadership, Legitimacy and Populist Politics*. Ed. Anton Allahar. Kingston: Ian Randle Publishers, 2001. 33–71. Print.

Watson, Hilbourne. "The Globalization of the Discourse on Gender and Its Impacts on the Caribbean." *The Culture of Gender and Sexuality in the Caribbean*. Ed. Linden Lewis. Florida: U P of Florida, 2003. 53–93. Print.

Williams Ntiri, Daphne. "Introduction." *Africana Womanism: Reclaiming Ourselves*. Ed. Clenora Hudsom-Weems. Oxon: Routledge, 2020. 1–8. Print.

Wilson, Kathleen. *The Island Race: Englishness, Empire and Gender in the Eighteenth Century*. New York: Routledge, 2003. Print.

Zakaria, Rafia. *Against White Feminism: Notes on Disruption*. New York: W. W. Norton & Company, 2021.

Index

Note: **Bold** page numbers refer to tables and page numbers followed by "n" denote endnotes.

abortion 10; spontaneous 58
abuse 4, 31, 43, 53, 57, 58, 76, 100; family 78; financial 60, 81; physical 59; sexual 10, 18, 26, 37, 57, 60, 85, 89, 96
Adams, Grantley 48
African retentions 11, 29
Afrofuturism 86
Alexander, Elizabeth 40
American War 21
Anglophone Caribbean 3
anti-patriarchal relationships 84–102
Arthur, Owen Seymour 78
autonomy 1, 13, 26, 28–30, 36, 53, 100; bodily 23, 37; dehumanization 20; deprivation of 20; sexual 53

Baptist, Edward 10
Barbados 1, 9–15, 18, 24, 43; childcare agency 58; Domestic Violence Protection Orders Act (1992) 79, 80; economics of 10; gender war 9; heterosexual relations 64; independence project 18; internal racial tensions 66; International Monetary Fund 78; juridical system 79; masculinity 54; Minors Act (1891) 55; national imagination 77; racial relations 40; sex work 36; slavery 25; Status of Children Act (1979) 55; womanhood 9
Barrow, Errol 47, 69, 77, 78
Bastardry Laws (1800) 16, 55
Beckford, George 18, 20
Beckles, Hilary 1, 2, 10, 11, 13, 25, 31–6, 40, 53, 95, 96, 103n10, 103n11
belief systems 69
Bermuda 10
Berry, Daina 38
biological difference 1, 92
Black boyhood 27
Black liberation 13, 45, 75
Black manhood 16, 28, 43
Black masculinity 26, 43, 67, 81
Black men: Black women and 7, 9–11, 16, 17; gender and sexuality performances 11; ideological unification of 69; individualistic patriarchy and 25–6; labour and 27–8; plantation and 24–32; self-preservation 10
Black motherhood 1, 92, 97
Blackness 42, 54, 67, 74, 79, 101
Black race 67, 89
Black womanhood 1, 5, 6, 51, 52, 56, 61, 78, 89
Black womb 1, 24, 55
Black women 1–3, 6, 12, 64–82, 88, 97; Black men and 7, 9–11, 16, 17; brutality of 10, 13; business coach 35; businesswoman (Phibbah) 33–7; constitutive negation 55; cook 35; entertainer 35; executive assistant 35; freedom of movement 1; gender and sexuality performances 11; hegemony 22; higgler 35; logistics handler 35; manager 35; masculine femininity 12; plantation and 32–7; power and agency 13; refusal to marry 11; seamstress 34; sexual labour 31; small loans financier 35
bourgeoisie 19, 46

Bradshaw, Robert 48
Brathwaite, Kamau 21, 36, 46, 85
breeders 30, 36
British Caribbean 3
British monarchy 18
Brody, Eugene: *Sex Contraception and Motherhood in Jamaica* 49
brutality 2, 10, 13, 20, 23, 87, 90, 101; greed and 87; sexual 36; slavery 40; of white men 20; of white women 31
Burnard, Trevor 11, 17n4, 20, 26, 28–30, 33, 35, 37, 391 *Mastery, Tyranny and Desire* 17n4, 33, 41n3
Bustamante, Alexander 48
Butch heterosexuality 2, 3, 8, 16, 17, 23, 30, 41, 42, 50–2, 61, 64–82, 99; legitimacy of 88; plantocratic patriarchal culture 33; self-sufficiency 34; trauma-informed relationships **71–2**
butchness 42, 89, 99; complexities of 73; definition of 50
Butler, Judith 12, 17, 90–2, 94, 96, 101, 102n3; *Gender Trouble* 92, 94
Butler, Uriah 48
Byrd, William 38

Canada: Diaspora communities 4; Indigenous populations 67; post-COVID 13
capitalism 47, 67, 68, 77, 78, 82; patriarchy and 82; racial 66, 84
Caribbean 1–4, 42, 68; culture of 33, 42, 43, 68; economic life of 9; gender studies 4, 43, 95; heterosexual orientation 3; intellectual tradition 7; nationalism 47–8; political process 68; pride 42; slave enterprise 11
Caribbean Court of Justice (CCJ) 79, 80
Caribbean society 18, 28, 56; contemporary 18, 28; feature of 19; governmental system 46; strong women and 48–54
Caribbean women 2–4, 6, 12–14, 87; dehumanization 40; detriment of 21; fake personhood 54; objectification 40
CARICOM ten-point plan 65–7
case studies, family and gender 56–61
charismatic leadership 69, 77, 78
Chevannes, Barry 13
Christianity 32, 75
Cipriani, C. C. 14
cisgenderism 52
citizenship 15, 77; plantation values 16; political 66; racialization 65; rights 55, 64, 65, 69; sociocultural 81
Civil Rights Movement 96
Clarke, Edith 49, 79; *My Mother Who Fathered Me* 49
class relations 16, 65
colonialism 47, 48, 66, 70, 76
colonization 9, 15, 43, 74
colouring box theory 5
colourism 34, 66, 97
Commonwealth Caribbean (CC) 1–4, 6, 9–15, 18, 21, 24, 43, 46, 47, 64, 84; gender reformation 9; gender relations 84; heterosexual relations 64; politourgeoise 66; polygamy 28, 29; queer people 64; slavery 25
compulsory heterosexuality 12, 91, 94, 95, 99
constitutive negation 54, 55, 65, 66
coupling separation 13
Crookshanks, William 23, 24
cultural hegemony 18

decolonizing process 69
Degruy, Joy 70
dehumanization 24, 40, 43, 90, 96; of Black people 20, 21; marker of 92; subjugation and 26; Transatlantic 95
depravity 24, 42
Diaspora 4
Domestic Violence Protection Order Act 79, 98
Downes, Aviston 47
Downs, Jim 40
Downs, Tim 86
Dunn, Richard 27
dysfunction 28–30, 42–62, 65

Eliss, Patricia 68
emancipation 3, 43, 44, 46; *see also* legal emancipation
emotional needs 20, 22
employment 14, 20, 53
Engels, Friedrich 93
Equiano, Olaudah 38
Erotic Defiance (Bryant) 75
Exceptional Violence (Thomas) 43, 65

fake personhood 54
family 15, 42, 43; abuse 78; court and gender 43, 60, 79, 103n8; dysfunction

42–62; instability 18, 56; patriarchal 91; structures 79, 93; values 32; violence 16
Fanon, Frantz 26
female embodiment 50
female masculinities 2, 5, 16, 85, 86, 89, 90, 95, 98, 99, 101, 102; characteristics of 49; heterosexual orientation 86
femininity 2, 11, 17, 25, 40, 72, 73, 76, 86, 90, 95; masculine 12, 50, 51; patriarchal constructions 100; self-identification 89; self-reliance and sex 36; social negotiation 89
feminism 1, 4–6, 15, 23, 32, 64, 71, 73, 74, 86, 87, 92, 101
feminists 1, 5, 14, 32, 73
Fog Olwig, Karen 97, 98
Foster, Thomas 24, 25, 32, 38
fraternity 87
Frazier, Franklin 47
freedom of movement 1–2

Garrigus, John 11
gender 1, 5; binary 2, 4, 6, 50; differentiation 70; expressions 70; identities 51, 98; justice 73–5; normativity 52; norms 1, 4, 12, 18, 87; performances 3–5, 10–12, 33, 40, 66, 72; ratooning 9–15, 53; separation 70; sexuality and 52; slavery, politics of 44; social construction of 3, 16, 91, 92, 96, 97; subjugation 36; theory 64, 73–5; trauma 70; values 10; wars 1, 3, 9, 94
gender relations 8, 9, 11, 38, 51, 60, 71, 74, 85; complexity of 14; heteronormative 84; reconciliation of 68; tense and acrimonious 15
Gender Trouble (Butler) 92, 94
Ghana 69
Glymph, Thavolia 32
Gomes, Albert 48
Government Industrial School 18, 60
Gramsci, Antonio 18
Gregg, Veronica 48, 51, 54–6, 63n2

Halberstam, Jack 2, 17, 50, 52, 63n5, 85, 94, 98, 99, 101, 102
Hall, Catherine 32
Hall, Douglas 17n4, 20, 24, 32, 33, 35, 40; *In Miserable Slavery* 17n4, 33, 41n2
Hamilton, Jill 14
Harris, Leslie 38
Hartman, Saidiya: *Lose Your Mother: A Journey Along the Atlantic Slave Route* 10
healing 17, 84–102
hegemonies 22; cultural 18; deconstruction of 73; knowledge 73; masculinity 24
Henry, Paget 9
heterosexual coupling 81, 82
heterosexual gratification 51
heterosexuality 12, 50, 65, 87; compulsory 12, 91, 94, 95, 99; *see also* Butch heterosexuality
heterosexual partnerships 3, 69, 84–102
heterosexual relations 64, 70, 89
Hudson-Weems, Clenora 74, 75

Iantaffi, Alex 70
independence 1, 19, 47, 53, 66, 69; movement 69; project 18
Indigenous populations 9, 67
individualistic patriarchy 21–3, 33, 42, 43, 61, 65, 71, 74, 79, 80, 92; Black men and 25–6; Caribbean nationalism and 47–8; multi-partnering 29; to proto-patriarchy 39; state formation and 43–8
inferior masculinity 45
In Miserable Slavery (Hall) 17n4, 33, 41n2
International Monetary Fund (IMF) 78
In the Castle of My Skin (Lamming) 47
intimate partner violence 60, 89, 103n9

Jamaica 3, 10, 21, 32, 39, 77; International Monetary Fund 78; legitimacy 13; marginalization 44; patriarchalism 39; violence 43
Jeffers, Audrey 14
Jefferson, Thomas 38
Jemmott, Jenny 46
Johnson, Jessica Marie 52, 53; *Wicked Flesh: Black WOmen, Intimacy and Freedom in the Atlantic World* 52
Joshua, Ebenezer 48

Keating, AnaLouise 7, 17n2, 84
Knight, Franklin 3, 4
knowledge: hegemonies 73; reification 8

labour 1, 16, 45, 68; Black men and 27–8; emotional 22, 24, 35; physical 54; sexual distribution 12
LaFont, Suzanne 60, 79, 94, 103n8
Lamming, George: *In the Castle of My Skin* 47
legal emancipation 9, 32, 43, 45, 96; first ratooning (1600) 10–12; Uprisings second ratooning (1930s) 12–14; Uprisings to Independence third ratooning (1930s) 14–15
legislation 55, 80
legitimacy 13, 40, 86, 88
Lerner, Gerda 20, 28
Lewis, Linden 90
Long, Edward 55
Lorde, Audre 2, 32, 49
Lose Your Mother: A Journey Along the Atlantic Slave Route (Hartman) 10

manhood 9, 15, 42, 53, 71, 76
Manley, Norman 48
marginalization theory 16, 43–5, 47
Marley, Bob 85
masculine femininity 12, 50, 51
masculinity 3, 7, 12, 17, 40, 44, 51, 54, 70, 72, 76; Black 26, 43, 67, 81; hegemonic 24; inferior 45; myth of 50; patriarchal 44, 45; white 30; *see also* female masculinities
Mastery, Tyranny and Desire (Burnard) 17n4, 33, 41n3
Mathurin-Mair, Lucille 2, 13, 15, 34, 41n4
matrilineality 54, 55, 98
Mauro, Anne 74, 76
Miller, Errol 16, 43–7
Minors Act (1891 in Barbados) 55
motherhood 10, 16, 54, 97
Mottley, Mia 82n3
multi-partnering 11, 28–30; individualistic patriarchy 29
Muslim 75
My Mother Who Fathered Me (Clarke) 49
Myrdal, Gunnar 47

nationalism 3, 47, 61, 66; reclaimed 75–81
Natural Rebels (Beckles) 33, 36, 53, 95
The Negro Family in British Guiana (Smith) 49
neo-colonialism 66
neoliberalism 66
North America 8, 47; farm work programmes 53

Onyeani, Chika 19, 67, 68
oppression 6, 40, 86, 95; gendered 9; racial 9, 99
Owens, Emily 38

Pateman, Carol 41n6, 65
paternalism 21, 39
patriarchal masculinity 44, 45
patriarchy 7, 15, 20, 39, 44, 74, 80, 82, 88, 101; development of 20; features of 20; legitimate 65, 95; traditional 45; Western 93; *see also* plantocratic patriarchal culture (PPC)
patronage 21, 47, 78
Patterson, Orlando 9–11, 46
Payne, Clement 48
Penn Handwerker, W.: *Women's Power and Social Revolution: Fertility Transition in the West Indies* 49
Phillips, Layli 5, 6
Pierre, Jemima 69
plantation 1, 9, 16; Black men and 24–32; Black women and 32–7; creation of 18–41; hierarchy 18; masculine femininity 12; race logics 66; as social theory 18; state/family dysfunction and 42–62; white men and 20–4; white women and 30–2
plantation society 1, 4, 11, 15, 20, 65; Blackness 54; brutality 2, 10; dysfunction 29; gender relations 11; hegemonic masculinity 24; human suffering 10; multi-partnering 11, 28; as polygamy 11; white men in 23
plantocratic patriarchal culture (PPC) 16, 20–2, 54, 55, 62, 65, 77, 80, 91, 98; Black women in 32, 33; Butch heterosexuality 33; definition of 21; features of **62**; logics of 47, 48; marriage, effect of 22–4; masculinity 45; womanhood 37
politics of inclusion 78
politourgeoisie 18, 19, 67, 69, 77, 78, 92
polygamy 11, 13, 28–30
Pooley, Sophia 31
Post Traumatic Slave Syndrome (Degruy) 38
poverty 42, 81
power relations 1, 14, 22, 73, 82, 97

PPC *see* plantocratic patriarchal culture (PPC)
privileges 6, 11, 14, 27; class 97; of heterosexuality 99; patriarchal 65; types of 19
property ownership restrictions 46
proto-patriarchy 39
psychological structures 96
Public Order Act (1970) 77

queerness 73, 75

race 1, 54, 73; Black 67, 89; liberation 68; reconciling 65–70; social construction of 16
racial capitalism 66, 84
racism 66
Randolph, James 31
ratoons of gender 9–15, 53
reconciling race 65–70
Reddock, Rhoda 12–14; *Women, Labour and Politics in Trinidad and Tobago* 13
religious fundamentalism 75
Reluctant Matriarchs 15, 34
reparative justice 65, 68
resentment 37, 72
resilience 15, 40, 42, 51, 101
resistance 3, 5, 7, 11, 52, 74, 88
Riley, Tarus 85
Robertson, Glory 63n3
Rodney, Walter 11

Saini, Angela 44
self-deprecation 85, 92
self-preservation 10
self-sufficiency 34, 36
sex 1–3, 10, 16, 21, 24, 40, 65, 100; forced 37; interracial 54; opposite 70, 95; social construction of 16; transactional 11; work 36
Sex Contraception and Motherhood in Jamaica (Brody) 49
sexual/sexuality: abuse 10, 18, 26, 37, 57, 60, 85, 89, 96; agency 32, 91; contact 38, 40; freedom 13, 28, 53; harassment 76; needs 22; orientation 3, 50, 101; predation 24, 37; vulnerability 96
Sheller, Mimi 17n3
Shepherd, Verene 13
Silvera, Makeda 49, 50
Simmons, Aishah 96
slavery 1, 2, 8, 14, 24, 29, 38, 92; Barbados 25; Black people 20; brutality of 40; enterprise 20; gender politics of 44; immoral consequences 38; psychological effects of 25; subjugation of 46; Transatlantic 20, 24, 47, 70, 86; United States 10
Smith, Raymond 10; *The Negro Family in British Guiana* 49
social construction of gender 3, 16, 91, 92, 96, 97
social justice 4, 5, 7, 84; actors 78; movements 6
social self 16
Spooner, Mary 79
state formation 43–8
state mechanics, women and men 54–6
Status of Children Act (1979 in Barbados) 55
Steadman, John 38
Stevenson, Brenda 38, 39
stewardship 39
stratification 65, 87; class 79; hierarchical 1
strong women 48–54
subjugation 15, 19, 20, 29, 46, 52, 62, 65, 75, 89, 95; dehumanization and 26; economic 9; gender 36; racial 20, 36; of slavery 46; terror and 24
survival mechanism 12, 97

Thistlewood, Thomas 7, 20–4, 26–8, 30, 32–5, 37, 38, 40, 42, 65, 66, 87, 92
Thomas, Deborah 3, 43, 47, 48, 81; *Exceptional Violence* 43, 65
threshold theories 7
toxic masculinity 88
Transatlantic dehumanization 95
Transatlantic kidnapping 81
Transatlantic slave trade 2, 42, 69
trauma 7, 29; effects of 81; emotional 30; gender 70; generational 40; racial 73; of rape 96; of sexual violence 96
trauma-informed partnerships 70–4, 82, 99
trauma-informed relationship **71–2**
Trouillot, Michel-Rolph 2
Truth, Sojourner 32, 86
two-handed reading 7, 8, 11, 14, 16, 22, 32, 39, 48, 54, 55, 66, 78

unemployment 14
United Nations 7, 73; CAP 130A 80; Decade of Women 4, 7
United States 4, 31, 32, 38; Black liberation struggles 45; marriages 39; slavery 10

Vasconcellos, Colleen 32
Victorianism 71
violence 37, 65, 80; colonial 7; contemporary 43; family 16; gender-based 87; intimate partner 60, 89, 103n9; patriarchal power 44; psychological 25; sexual 25, 96

Walcott, Renaldo 46
Walker, Alice 5, 73, 87
wandering law 18
Western colonization 65
West Indies 3, 98
white men 10, 14, 18, 26, 30, 32; plantation and 20–4; slavery 29
white supremacy 5, 23, 25, 30, 73
white womanhood 1, 89
white women 20, 23, 24; hegemony 22; marriage possibilities 22; plantation and 30–2
Wicked Flesh: Black WOmen, Intimacy and Freedom in the Atlantic World (Johnson) 52
William, Rose 36
womanhood 2–4, 6, 9, 12, 13, 15, 25, 30, 34, 36, 42, 49, 50, 54, 73, 84, 89, 92, 99; Black femme performances of 53; dominant performance of 53; gender performance of 66; masculine performance 16; monolithic construction of 5; negotiations of 7; non-traditional performances 41; plantocratic patriarchal culture 37; recalibration of 7; reclamation of 52; transgressive 51
womanism 5, 64, 73, 74, 87; definition of 6; features of 5
womanness 88
Women, Labour and Politics in Trinidad and Tobago (Reddock) 13
Women's Power and Social Revolution: Fertility Transition in the West Indies (Penn Handwerker) 49

For Product Safety Concerns and Information please contact our EU representative GPSR@taylorandfrancis.com
Taylor & Francis Verlag GmbH, Kaufingerstraße 24, 80331 München, Germany

www.ingramcontent.com/pod-product-compliance
Ingram Content Group UK Ltd.
Pitfield, Milton Keynes, MK11 3LW, UK
UKHW021245190926
475569UK00001BA/10
9781032855691